Campbell's

SIMPLY DELICIOUS
RECIPES

BRIMAR

NOTE: CAMPBELL'S CONDENSED SOUP CAN SIZES USED IN THIS BOOK

1 CAN = 295 g (*10.4 oz*)

Published in 1992 by **BRIMAR PUBLISHING INC.**
338 St. Antoine Street East
Montreal, Canada H2Y 1A3
Tel.: (514) 954-1441
Fax: (514) 954-1443

Editor: Angela Rahaniotis
Graphic Design and Layout: Zapp
Photography: Michel Bodson
Food Preparation: Chef Stephane Drouin
Stylist: Muriel Bodson
Accessories courtesy of Potpourri, Pier 1 Imports,
Les Carreaux Ramca Ltd., La Baie.

This edition was produced by Campbell Soup Company's Publications Center, Campbell Soup Company, Campbell Place, Camden, New Jersey 08103-1799, U.S.A.

Campbell's SIMPLY DELICIOUS RECIPES
Corporate Editor: Patricia Teberg
Assistant Editors: Alice Joy Carter, Margaret Romano
Editorial Assistant: Gloria J. Pinchac
United Kingdom Consultant: Justine Dickenson
Creative Director: Stacy-Jo Mannella

Every recipe in Campbell's SIMPLY DELICIOUS RECIPES cookbook was developed and tested in the Campbell Kitchens by professional home economists.

"Campbell International" is a division of Campbell Soup Company. All of the recipes in Campbell's SIMPLY DELICIOUS RECIPES cookbook have been adapted for use by consumers in the United Kingdom. Any questions about Campbell's Soups should be directed to: Campbell Grocery Products Ltd., Hardwick Road, King's Lynn, Norfolk PE30 4HS, England. Or write to: Campbell International, Campbell Soup Company, Campbell Place, Camden, New Jersey, 08103-1799, U.S.A.

Pictured on the front cover, starting clockwise from top left: Creamy Chicken with Mushrooms *(see recipe, page 71)*; Creamy Potato Bake *(see recipe, page 151)*; and Lasagne *(see recipe, page 75)*.

Microwave Cooking Times: Microwave cooking times in this book are approximate. These recipes have been tested in 650- to 700-watt microwave ovens. Foods cooked in lower-wattage ovens may require longer cooking times. Use the cooking times as guidelines and check for doneness before adding more time.

Preparation and Cooking Times: The preparation times are based on the approximate amount of time required to assemble the recipe *before* baking or cooking. These times include preparation steps such as chopping; mixing; cooking rice, pasta, vegetables; etc. The fact that some preparation steps can be done simultaneously is taken into account. The cook times are based on the minimum amount of time required to cook, bake or grill the food in the recipes.

ISBN 2-89433-023-5
Printed in Canada

Campbell's

SIMPLY DELICIOUS RECIPES

Let cooking with Campbell's condensed Soups be your recipe for success. All the great-tasting recipes in SIMPLY DELICIOUS RECIPES rely on flavourful, high-quality Campbell's Soups to make cooking easy — with delicious results!

Inside, you'll find more than 125 kitchen-tested recipes, from tempting appetizers and hearty stews to savoury main dishes and tasty vegetables. The more than 150 beautiful photographs, including many step-by-step techniques, will whet your appetite and inspire you to start cooking.

Everyone at Campbell believes that great-tasting recipes begin with Campbell's Soups. From our Kitchens to yours, we hope your family and friends will enjoy these Campbell favourites!

Campbell's family of cooking soups from around the world

Campbell's® Soups bring more than 125 great-tasting recipes to you

COOKING WITH CAMPBELL'S SOUPS — IT'S EASY

Get a head start in the kitchen and begin with Campbell's condensed Soups. It's the real secret to making delicious meals in minutes. Campbell's condensed Soups make cooking easy for new and experienced cooks alike, and the rich concentrated flavour eliminates the need for lots of extra ingredients.

- Campbell's condensed Soups can be used as sauces or dips, bases for casseroles and for adding flavour to home-made soups.
- When making soup, dilute the soup to the desired consistency with milk, stock, sherry, wine, water or other liquids of your choice. Combine the soup with the liquid gradually, stirring well to mix evenly. Then, heat the soup until heated through — never boil as it overheats and may impair the quality of the soup.
- In recipes, often one variety of soup can be substituted for another so ring the changes with your own favourites.

TRY THESE GREAT-TASTING IDEAS:

Souper Sauces: Dilute any condensed soup with up to 150 ml (¼ pt) liquid and add a little seasoning, if liked. Mustard, horseradish sauce, spices, herbs, soy sauce or grated cheese can all be stirred into the soup for extra flavour. Serve over fried or grilled meat, poultry and fish. Alternatively use as a baked potato or toast topping.

Casseroles and Stews: For really creamy casseroles and stews, cook meat and poultry on the hob or in the oven with Campbell's condensed Soup. Dilute the soup with between 150 ml (¼ pt) and 300 ml (½ pt) liquid before adding meat, vegetables and/or pasta. Simmer gently and stir occasionally to prevent sticking. Condensed vegetable soup should be added near the end of the cooking time as the vegetables are already cooked.

Vegetables: Serve freshly cooked vegetables with a tasty sauce made from Campbell's condensed Soup diluted to the desired consistency with milk. Alternatively cook frozen vegetables in undiluted soup until tender.

Pasta: Campbell's condensed Soups are ideal for tossing with freshly cooked pasta. Heat the soup through gently and season to taste. Add pasta and toss to coat, diluting with milk or water, if liked. For a quick pasta au gratin, spoon pasta mixture into a flame-proof dish, sprinkle with grated cheese and grill until golden.

Rice: Cook rice in Campbell's condensed Consommé diluted with water for extra flavour. Cream soups can be diluted with water and added to rice to make rich tasting risottos and pilafs.

Home-Made Soups: Just combine different varieties of Campbell's condensed Soup, adding your favourite vegetables, pasta, cooked poultry or meat, or canned fish.

Dips: Make a quick party dip by adding sour cream or fromage frais to Campbell's condensed Soup. If liked, stir in desired seasoning, crushed garlic and/or chopped fresh herbs. Serve with vegetables or bread sticks.

Campbell's
SIMPLY DELICIOUS
RECIPES

BASIL CHICKEN AND BROCCOLI POTATO TOPPER

1 can	**CAMPBELL'S condensed Cream of Chicken Soup**
75 g	**(*3 oz*) full fat soft cheese**
175 g	**(*6 oz*) cubed, cooked chicken**
175 g	**(*6 oz*) frozen broccoli florets**
30 ml	**(*2 tbsp*) milk**
5 ml	**(*1 tsp*) dried basil**
5 ml	**(*1 tsp*) lemon juice**
4	**hot baked potatoes, halved**
	Chopped red pepper for garnish

■ In medium saucepan over moderate heat, combine soup, soft cheese, chicken, broccoli, milk, basil and lemon juice. Heat through, stirring occasionally.

■ Spoon over potatoes. Garnish with red pepper, if liked.

To microwave: In medium microwave-proof dish, combine soup, cheese, chicken, broccoli, milk, basil and lemon juice. Cover; microwave on HIGH 8 minutes, stirring halfway through heating. Continue as directed above.

Basil Chicken and Asparagus: Prepare Basil Chicken and Broccoli as above, *except* substitute 1 packet 250 g (*8.8 oz*) frozen asparagus spears, cut into 2.5-cm (*1-in*) pieces, for the broccoli florets.

Serves 4.
Prep Time: 10 minutes
Cook Time: 10 minutes plus baking potatoes

BASIL CHICKEN AND BROCCOLI POTATO TOPPER

ARTICHOKE-CHILLI DIP

1 can	**CAMPBELL'S condensed Cream of Celery *or* Cream of Chicken Soup**
175 g	**(*6 oz*) full fat soft cheese, softened**
1 can (398 g)	**(*14 oz*) artichoke hearts, rinsed, drained and chopped**
1	**green chilli, de-seeded and finely chopped**
40 g	**(*1½ oz*) grated Parmesan cheese**
	Paprika

■ Preheat oven to 190 °C (*375 °F, gas mark 5*). Meanwhile, in 1.15-Lt (*2-pt*) ovenproof dish, stir soup and soft cheese until well combined. Stir in artichokes, chilli and Parmesan cheese.

■ Bake 15 minutes or until hot and bubbling. Stir; sprinkle with paprika. Serve with *crackers* or *tortilla chips* for dipping.

To microwave: In 1.15-Lt (*2-pt*) microwave-proof dish, stir soup and soft cheese until well combined. Stir in artichokes, chilli and Parmesan cheese. Microwave, uncovered, on HIGH 6 minutes or until hot, stirring twice during cooking. Sprinkle with paprika. Serve as directed above.

Serves 6 to 8.
Prep Time: 10 minutes
Cook Time: 15 minutes

DILLED SALMON DIP

1 can	**CAMPBELL'S condensed Cream of Celery *or* Cream of Chicken Soup**
45 ml	**(*3 tbsp*) mayonnaise *or* sour cream**
30 ml	**(*2 tbsp*) prepared horseradish sauce**
15 ml	**(*1 tbsp*) chopped fresh dill *or* 5 ml (*1 tsp*) dried dill weed**
	Salt *and* ground black pepper
1 can (213 g)	**(*7½ oz*) salmon, drained and flaked**
	Fresh chopped dill *and* dill sprig for garnish

■ In medium bowl, combine soup, mayonnaise, horseradish sauce and chopped dill. Add salmon; mix lightly. Season to taste with salt and pepper. Cover; refrigerate 15 minutes.

■ To serve: Garnish dip with additional dill, if liked. Serve with *assorted cut-up vegetables* and *rye bread* for dipping.

Serves 6 to 8.
Prep Time: 10 minutes
Chill Time: 15 minutes

MINI BROCCOLI PIZZAS

150 g	**(*5 oz*) small broccoli florets**
1	**small red pepper, de-seeded and cut into strips**
1 can	**CAMPBELL'S condensed Cream of Mushroom Soup**
1.2 ml	**(*¼ tsp*) garlic granules (optional)**
1.2 ml	**(*¼ tsp*) dried Italian seasoning**
6	**English muffins, halved and toasted**
225 g	**(*8 oz*) mozzarella cheese, grated**

■ Preheat oven to 190 °C (*375 °F, gas mark 5*). Meanwhile, in small saucepan over moderate heat, in boiling water, gently simmer broccoli and red pepper 3 minutes. Drain well; set aside.

■ In small bowl, combine soup, garlic granules and Italian seasoning. Spread soup mixture evenly over 12 muffin halves; place on baking sheets.

■ Top each with cooked broccoli and red pepper. Sprinkle with mozzarella cheese. Bake 10 minutes or until cheese melts. Serve immediately.

TIP: These individual broccoli pizzas are easy to assemble. Choose from a variety of toppers such as: sliced pepperoni, chopped artichoke hearts, chopped prawns, sliced spring onions and sliced olives.

Makes 12 mini pizzas.
Prep Time: 15 minutes
Cook Time: 10 minutes

MUSTARD CHICKEN BITES

1 can	**CAMPBELL'S condensed Cream of Chicken Soup**
30 ml	(*2 tbsp*) **Dijon mustard**
15 ml	(*1 tbsp*) **chopped fresh dill** *or* **5 ml** (*1 tsp*) **dried dill weed**
5 ml	(*1 tsp*) **lemon juice**
2	**cloves garlic, peeled and crushed**
675 g	(*1½ lb*) **boneless chicken breasts, skinned, cut into 2.5-cm** (*1-in*) **cubes**
45 ml	(*3 tbsp*) **milk**
	Fresh dill *and* **lemon slices for garnish**

■ In large bowl, combine soup, mustard, dill, lemon juice and garlic. Reserve *100 ml* (*4 fl oz*) of soup mixture for dipping sauce. Add chicken to remaining soup mixture; toss to coat well. Cover; refrigerate 2 hours.

■ On skewers, thread chicken. Place skewers on grill pan. Place under preheated medium grill 10 minutes or until chicken is golden brown and tender, turning often. Remove chicken from skewers. Arrange chicken on serving plate; keep warm.

■ Meanwhile, in small saucepan over moderate heat, stir together reserved soup mixture and milk; heat through. Serve as dipping sauce with grilled chicken. Garnish with dill and lemon, if liked.

Makes about 50 appetizers.
Prep Time: 15 minutes
Marinating Time: 2 hours
Cook Time: 8 to 10 minutes

1 In large bowl, combine soup, mustard, dill, lemon juice and garlic.

MUSTARD CHICKEN BITES

2 Add chicken to remaining soup mixture.

3 Thread chicken on skewers.

4 Turn chicken skewers to brown all sides.

CRAB PARMESAN TOASTS

CRAB PARMESAN TOASTS

1 can	**CAMPBELL'S condensed Cream of Mushroom Soup**
2 cans (170 g each)	**(6 oz each) crabmeat, drained**
50 g	**(2 oz) chopped, trimmed celery**
2	**spring onions, trimmed and sliced**
½	**lemon rind, finely grated**
15 ml	**(1 tbsp) lemon juice**
1	**loaf French bread (about 40 cm / 16 in long)**
40 g	**(1½ oz) finely grated Parmesan cheese**
	Paprika

■ In medium bowl, combine soup, crabmeat, celery, onions, lemon rind and lemon juice.

■ Diagonally slice bread into 16 slices. Arrange on 2 baking sheets. Place under preheated medium grill 2 minutes, turning once, until toasted.

■ Spread crab mixture on *each* bread slice. Sprinkle with Parmesan and paprika.

■ Place under preheated medium grill 5 minutes or until lightly browned. Serve immediately.

Makes 16 appetizers.
Prep Time: 15 minutes
Cook Time: 10 minutes

BARBECUE PORK POTATO TOPPER

15 ml	**(1 tbsp) vegetable oil**
1	**medium onion, thinly sliced**
225 g	**(8 oz) boneless pork, cut into very thin strips**
1 can	**CAMPBELL'S condensed Cream of Tomato Soup**
30 ml	**(2 tbsp) water**
15 ml	**(1 tbsp) light brown soft sugar**
15 ml	**(1 tbsp) malt vinegar**
10 ml	**(2 tsp) Worcestershire sauce**
4	**hot baked potatoes, halved**

■ In large frying pan over moderate heat, in hot oil, gently fry onion until golden brown and softened. Push onion to one side, add pork; gently fry until browned. Spoon off fat.

■ Stir in soup, water, sugar, vinegar and Worcestershire sauce. Simmer gently 5 minutes. Spoon mixture over potatoes.

Serves 4.
Prep Time: 10 minutes
Cook Time: 15 minutes plus baking potatoes

MEXICAN-STYLE BEEF POTATO TOPPER

15 ml	(*1 tbsp*) vegetable oil
1	medium onion, cut into wedges
1	small green pepper, de-seeded and cut into strips
225 g	(*8 oz*) rump steak, cut into very thin strips
1 can	CAMPBELL'S condensed Cream of Mushroom Soup
60 ml	(*4 tbsp*) water
10 ml	(*2 tsp*) lime juice
2.5 ml	(*½ tsp*) dried oregano
1.2 ml	(*¼ tsp*) ground cumin
4	hot baked potatoes, halved
	Salsa *or* taco sauce

■ In large frying pan over moderate heat, in hot oil, gently fry onion and green pepper until vegetables are browned and tender. Push vegetables to one side, add beef; gently fry until browned. Spoon off fat.

■ Stir in soup, water, lime juice, oregano and cumin. Heat through, stirring occasionally. Spoon mixture over potatoes. Top with salsa.

Serves 4.
Prep Time: 15 minutes
Cook Time: 10 minutes

CREAMY CHICKEN VOL AU VENTS

1 can	**CAMPBELL'S condensed Chicken & Mushroom Soup**
175 g	**(*6 oz*) diced, cooked chicken**
45 ml	**(*3 tbsp*) milk**
15 ml	**(*1 tbsp*) fresh parsley (optional)**
	Salt *and* ground black pepper
36	**frozen medium vol au vent cases, freshly baked**

■ In large bowl, combine soup, chicken, milk and parsley. Season to taste with salt and pepper. Spoon into vol au vent cases.

Hot Creamy Chicken Vol au Vents: Prepare Creamy Chicken Vol au Vents as directed above, *except* in large saucepan, combine soup, chicken, milk and parsley. Over moderate heat, heat through. Season to taste with salt and pepper. Spoon into vol au vent cases.

Makes 36 appetizers.
Prep Time: 25 minutes

HERB CHEESECAKE

675 g	(*1½ lb*) full fat soft cheese, softened
600 ml	(*1 pt*) sour cream, divided
1 can	CAMPBELL'S condensed Cream of Celery Soup
3	(size 3) eggs
40 g	(*1½ oz*) grated Parmesan cheese
2	cloves garlic, peeled and crushed
15 ml	(*1 tbsp*) cornflour
30 ml	(*2 tbsp*) finely chopped fresh basil *or* 10 ml (*2 tsp*) dried basil
15 ml	(*1 tbsp*) finely chopped fresh thyme *or* 5 ml (*1 tsp*) dried thyme
5 ml	(*1 tsp*) finely chopped fresh tarragon *or* 1.2 ml (*¼ tsp*) dried tarragon
2.5 ml	(*½ tsp*) ground black pepper
	Red pepper strips, lemon peel twists *and* assorted fresh herbs for garnish
	Crackers, melba toast *or* fresh cut-up vegetables

■ Preheat oven to 180 °C (*350 °F, gas mark 4*). Lightly grease 23-cm (*9-in*) springclip cake tin.

■ In food processor or large mixing bowl, combine soft cheese, *300 ml* (*½ pt*) of sour cream and soup. Blend mixture in food processor or beat with electric mixer at medium speed until smooth. Add eggs, Parmesan cheese, garlic, cornflour, basil, thyme, tarragon and ground black pepper. Blend or beat until smooth. Turn into prepared pan and place on baking tray.

■ Bake 1 hour or until light brown (top may crack). Turn off oven; let stand in oven 30 minutes more. Cool in pan on wire rack. Cover; refrigerate at least 4 hours or overnight before serving.

■ Spread remaining sour cream over cheesecake. Garnish with red pepper, lemon twists and assorted fresh herbs, if liked. Serve with crackers.

Serves 10 to 12.
Prep Time: 20 minutes
Cook Time: 1 hour
Chill Time: 4 hours or overnight

HERB CHEESECAKE

$\mathcal{F}$LORENTINE PARTY APPETIZERS

4	**(size 3) eggs, beaten**
250 g	**(*9 oz*) mature Cheddar cheese spread, softened**
1 can	**CAMPBELL'S condensed Cream of Mushroom Soup**
450 g	**(*1 lb*) frozen chopped spinach, thawed, *well drained* and finely chopped**
1 can (227 g)	**(*8 oz*) water chestnuts, drained and chopped**
2	**spring onions, trimmed and chopped**
1 tube (308 g)	**refrigerated croissants (6 ready-to-bake croissants)**

■ Preheat oven to 180 °C (*350 °F, gas mark 4*).

■ In large bowl, beat eggs and cheese spread. Add soup. Stir in spinach, water chestnuts and spring onions; mix well.

■ Unroll croissants, but *do not separate*. Press onto base of 33- by 23-cm (*13- by 9-in*) greased Swiss roll tin. Gently press seams together. Spread spinach mixture over dough.

■ Bake 40 minutes or until knife inserted in centre comes out clean. Let stand 10 minutes before cutting. Cut into 4-cm (*1½-in*) pieces.

Makes 40 appetizers.
Prep Time: 20 minutes
Cook Time: 40 minutes

1 Add spinach, water chestnuts and spring onions to soup-cheese mixture; mix well.

2 Press croissants, without separating, onto base of greased Swiss roll tin.

3 Spread spinach mixture over dough.

FLORENTINE PARTY APPETIZERS

℘IZZA POTATO TOPPER

15 ml	(*1 tbsp*) vegetable oil
1	medium green pepper, de-seeded and chopped
2.5 ml	(*½ tsp*) dried basil
2.5 ml	(*½ tsp*) dried oregano
1 can	CAMPBELL'S condensed Cream of Tomato Soup
30 ml	(*2 tbsp*) water
75 g	(*3 oz*) pepperoni, halved lengthwise and sliced
4	hot baked potatoes, halved
	Grated mozzarella cheese

■ In medium saucepan over moderate heat, in hot oil, gently fry pepper, basil and oregano until pepper is tender. Stir in soup, water and pepperoni. Heat through, stirring occasionally.

■ Spoon mixture over potatoes. Top with mozzarella cheese.

To microwave: In medium microwave-proof dish, combine oil, pepper, basil and oregano. Cover; microwave on HIGH 4 minutes or until pepper is tender, stirring halfway through cooking. Stir in soup, water and pepperoni. Cover; microwave on HIGH 3 minutes or until hot. Continue as directed above.

Serves 4.
Prep Time: 10 minutes
Cook Time: 10 minutes plus baking potatoes

CREAMY MINCE POTATO TOPPER

450 g	(*1 lb*) **lean minced beef**
1	**small onion, chopped**
1	**clove garlic, peeled and crushed**
1 can	**CAMPBELL'S condensed Cream of Mushroom Soup**
2.5 ml	(*¹/₂ tsp*) **paprika**
150 ml	(*¹/₄ pt*) **sour cream**
6	**hot baked potatoes, halved**
	Chopped tomato
	Chopped fresh parsley

■ In large frying pan, over moderate heat, gently fry mince, onion and garlic until meat is well browned and onion is softened, stirring to separate meat. Spoon off fat. Stir in soup and paprika; simmer 15 minutes, stirring occasionally. Remove from heat. Stir in sour cream.

■ Spoon mixture over potatoes. Top with chopped tomato and parsley.

To microwave: In 2-Lt (*3¹/₂-pt*) microwave-proof dish, combine onion and garlic. Cover; microwave on HIGH 2 minutes, stirring halfway through cooking. Crumble mince into dish. Cover; microwave on HIGH 5 minutes or until meat is no longer pink, stirring halfway through cooking. Spoon off fat. Stir in soup and paprika. Cover; microwave on HIGH 3 minutes. Stir in sour cream. Continue as directed above.

Serves 6.
Prep Time: 5 minutes
Cook Time: 20 minutes

SOUTHWEST POTATO SOUP

15 g	**(½ oz) butter _or_ margarine**
4	**spring onions, trimmed and chopped**
1 can	**CAMPBELL'S condensed Cream of Celery Soup**
350 ml	**(12 fl oz) milk**
1	**medium potato, peeled, cooked and diced**
25 g	**(1 oz) Cheddar cheese, grated**

■ In medium saucepan over moderate heat, in hot butter, gently fry spring onions until softened, stirring occasionally.

■ Stir in soup, milk and potato. Heat through, stirring occasionally. Remove from heat. Add Cheddar cheese, stirring until cheese melts.

Serves 2 to 3 as a starter.
Prep Time: 15 minutes
Cook Time: 10 minutes

SWEETCORN CHOWDER

15 g	(*½ oz*) **butter** *or* **margarine**
1	**small onion, chopped**
½	**small green pepper, de-seeded and finely chopped**
2.5 ml	(*½ tsp*) **dried dill weed**
2 cans	**CAMPBELL'S condensed Cream of Celery Soup**
600 ml	(*1 pt*) **milk**
150 ml	(*¼ pt*) **water**
225 g	(*8 oz*) **frozen sweetcorn**
1	**medium potato, peeled, cooked and diced**
	Salt *and* **ground black pepper**

■ In large saucepan over moderate heat, in hot butter, gently fry onion, green pepper and dill until vegetables are softened.

■ Stir in soup, milk, water, sweetcorn and potato. Season to taste with salt and pepper. Heat to simmer, stirring occasionally. Reduce heat to low. Simmer gently 5 minutes. Garnish with *fresh dill,* if liked.

Serves 6 as a starter.
Prep Time: 15 minutes
Cook Time: 15 minutes

Tuna-Tortellini Soup

1 can	**CAMPBELL'S condensed Cream of Chicken Soup**
300 ml	**($\frac{1}{2}$ pt) chicken stock**
1.2 ml	**($\frac{1}{4}$ tsp) dried basil**
	Pinch garlic granules (optional)
250 g	**(9 oz) dried cheese-filled tortellini*, cooked and drained**
150 g	**(5 oz) frozen sweetcorn**
300 ml	**($\frac{1}{2}$ pt) milk**
1 can (198 g)	**(7 oz) tuna, drained**
1	**small green pepper, de-seeded and diced (optional)**
	Chopped fresh parsley for garnish

■ In large saucepan, combine soup, stock, basil and garlic. Cover; over high heat, heat to simmer.

■ Stir in pasta, sweetcorn, milk, tuna and green pepper; heat through, stirring occasionally. Garnish with parsley, if liked.

* If not available at your food store, substitute 75 g (3 oz) dried pasta twists, cooked and drained.

Serves 4 as a main dish.
Prep Time: 20 minutes
Cook Time: 15 minutes

VEGETABLE BEEF SOUP

2 cans	**CAMPBELL'S condensed Consommé**
300 ml	**(1/2 pt) water**
2	**medium potatoes, peeled and cubed**
450 g	**(1 lb) frozen mixed vegetables**
1 can (220 g)	**(8 oz) chopped tomatoes, undrained**
150 g	**(5 oz) cubed, cooked beef**
1.2 ml	**(1/4 tsp) dried thyme**
	Salt *and* ground black pepper

■ In large saucepan, combine consommé, water and potatoes. Over high heat, heat to simmer. Reduce heat to low. Cover; simmer gently 5 minutes.

■ Stir in frozen vegetables, tomatoes, beef and thyme. Season to taste with salt and pepper. Cover; heat to simmer. Simmer until vegetables are tender.

Serves 4 to 6 as a starter.
Prep Time: 10 minutes
Cook Time: 20 minutes

HAM BARLEY SOUP

40 g	(*1½ oz*) butter *or* margarine
75 g	(*3 oz*) button mushrooms, wiped and sliced
1	small onion, chopped
1.2 ml	(*¼ tsp*) dried thyme
50 g	(*2 oz*) pearl barley
300 ml	(*½ pt*) chicken stock
1 can	CAMPBELL'S condensed Consommé
300 ml	(*½ pt*) water
1.2 ml	(*¼ tsp*) ground black pepper
350 ml	(*12 fl oz*) milk
100 g	(*4 oz*) ham, cut into 4-cm (*1½-in*) matchstick-thin strips
150 g	(*5 oz*) frozen peas

■ In large saucepan over moderate heat, in hot butter, gently fry mushrooms, onion and thyme 3 minutes, stirring occasionally. Add barley gently fry 2 minutes or until golden, stirring regularly.

■ Stir in stock, consommé, water and pepper Cover; heat to simmer. Reduce heat to low. Simmer gently 40 minutes, stirring occasionally.

■ Stir in milk, ham and peas. Simmer gently 5 minutes more or until barley is tender, stirring regularly.

Serves 4 as a main dish.
Prep Time: 10 minutes
Cook Time: 50 minutes

1 Gently fry mushrooms, onion and thyme, stirring occasionally.

2 Add barley and gently fry until golden.

HAM BARLEY SOUP

3 Add stock, con-
sommé, water and pepper.

4 Stir in milk, ham
and peas.

$\mathcal{R}$ATATOUILLE SOUP

1 can	**CAMPBELL'S condensed Tomato & Onion Soup**
450 ml	**(*¾ pt*) water**
100 g	**(*4 oz*) courgettes, trimmed and sliced**
1	**small yellow pepper, de-seeded and chopped**
1	**small red pepper, de-seeded and chopped**
15 g	**(*1 oz*) Cheddar cheese, grated**

■ In medium saucepan, combine soup and water. Stir in courgettes and peppers. Over moderate heat, heat to simmer.

■ Reduce heat to low. Simmer gently 20 minutes or until vegetables are tender. Sprinkle with Cheddar cheese just before serving.

Serves 3 to 4 as a starter.
Prep Time: 10 minutes
Cook Time: 25 minutes

CHILLI CON CARNE

450 g	(*1 lb*) minced beef
1	small onion, chopped
10 ml	(*2 tsp*) hot chilli powder
1	clove garlic, peeled and crushed
1 can (439 g)	(*15½ oz*) red kidney beans, undrained
1 can	CAMPBELL'S condensed Cream of Tomato Soup
60 ml	(*4 tbsp*) water
10 ml	(*2 tsp*) malt vinegar
	Freshly cooked rice (optional)

■ In large frying pan over moderate heat, gently fry mince, onion, chilli powder and garlic until meat is well browned and onion is softened, stirring to separate meat. Spoon off fat.

■ Stir in undrained beans, soup, water and vinegar. Heat to simmer. Reduce heat to low. Simmer gently 15 minutes, stirring occasionally.

■ Serve over rice, if liked.

To microwave: In 2-Lt (*3½-pt*) microwave-proof dish, crumble mince. Stir in onion, chilli powder and garlic. Cover; microwave on HIGH 5 minutes or until meat is no longer pink, stirring halfway through cooking to separate meat. Spoon off fat. Stir in beans, soup and vinegar. Cover; microwave on HIGH 5 minutes or until bubbling, stirring halfway through cooking.

Serves 4 as a main dish.
Prep Time: 10 minutes
Cook Time: 25 minutes

$\mathcal{D}$OWN-HOME VEGETABLE CHOWDER

25 g	(*1 oz*) butter *or* margarine
50 g	(*2 oz*) sliced, trimmed celery
2	spring onions, trimmed and sliced
1 can	CAMPBELL'S condensed Cream of Celery Soup
300 ml	(*½ pt*) milk
150 g	(*5 oz*) frozen sweetcorn
1	medium potato, peeled, cooked and diced
	Pinch ground black pepper

In medium saucepan over moderate heat, in hot butter, gently fry spring onions and celery until softened, stirring occasionally. Stir in soup, milk, sweetcorn, potato and pepper. Heat through, stirring regularly.

TIP: For added flavour, sprinkle crumbled cooked bacon, chopped spring onions and chopped red pepper on each serving.

Serves 2 to 3 as a starter.
Prep Time: 10 minutes
Cook Time: 10 minutes

CHICKEN AND SWEETCORN SOUP

1 can	**CAMPBELL'S condensed Chicken & Mushroom Soup**
300 ml	**(*1/2 pt*) water**
100 g	**(*4 oz*) diced, cooked chicken**
1/2	**red pepper, de-seeded and diced**
1 can (198 g)	**(*7 oz*) sweetcorn, drained**
30 ml	**(*2 tbsp*) dry sherry (optional)**

■ In medium saucepan combine soup and water. Add chicken, pepper, sweetcorn and sherry. Over moderate heat, heat to simmer.

■ Reduce heat to low. Simmer gently 8 to 10 minutes or until hot, stirring occasionally.

Serves 2 to 3 as a starter.
Prep Time: 10 minutes
Cook Time: 15 minutes

SPECIAL LEEK 'N' HAM SOUP

25 g	**(*1 oz*) butter *or* margarine**
275 g	**(*10 oz*) leeks, trimmed, washed and sliced**
1 can	**CAMPBELL'S condensed Ham & Cheese Soup**
300 ml	**(*1/2 pt*) milk**
150 ml	**(*1/4 pt*) dry white wine**

■ In large saucepan over moderate heat, in hot butter, gently fry leeks until softened.

■ Stir in soup, milk and wine. Heat to simmer. Reduce heat to low. Simmer gently 10 minutes, stirring occasionally.

Serves 4 as a starter.
Prep Time: 10 minutes
Cook Time: 20 minutes

PRAWN CREOLE SOUP

1 can	CAMPBELL'S condensed Cream of Tomato Soup
300 ml	(*1/2 pt*) water
1/2	green pepper, de-seeded and chopped
1/2	small onion, finely chopped
75 g	(*3 oz*) cooked long-grain rice
75 g	(*3 oz*) coarsely chopped, peeled prawns (thawed if frozen)
1.2 ml	(*1/4 tsp*) Tabasco sauce
	Fresh dill sprigs for garnish

■ In small saucepan, combine soup and water. Add pepper, onion, rice, prawns and Tabasco sauce. Over moderate heat, heat through, stirring occasionally. Garnish with dill, if liked.

Fish Creole Soup: Prepare Prawn Creole Soup as directed above, *except* substitute *1 small fish fillet,* cooked and flaked, for the prawns.

Serves 2 to 3 as a starter.
Prep Time: 10 minutes
Cook Time: 10 minutes

SAVOURY PORK STEW

0 ml	(*2 tbsp*) **vegetable oil**
50 g	(*1 lb*) **boneless pork, cut into 2-cm (3/4-in) pieces**
cans	**CAMPBELL'S condensed Cream of Celery Soup**
00 ml	(*1/2 pt*) **apple juice**
.2 ml	(*1/4 tsp*) **black pepper**
.2 ml	(*1/4 tsp*) **caraway seed**
	carrots, peeled and diagonally sliced
	medium red potatoes, scrubbed and cut into chunks
50 g	(*9 oz*) **roughly chopped white cabbage**
00 ml	(*4 fl oz*) **milk**

■ In large saucepan over moderate heat, in hot oil, gently fry pork until browned on all sides.

■ Add soup, apple juice, pepper and caraway. Heat to simmer. Reduce heat to low. Cover; simmer gently 30 minutes, stirring occasionally.

■ Add carrots and potatoes. Cover; simmer gently 10 minutes. Add cabbage. Cover; simmer gently 15 minutes or until vegetables are tender.

■ Add milk. Heat through, stirring regularly. *Do not boil.*

Serves 6 as a main dish.
Prep Time: 20 minutes
Cook Time: 1 hour

BUTTERNUT SQUASH BISQUE

450 g	(*1 lb*) butternut squash, peeled, de-seeded and cubed
25 g	(*1 oz*) butter *or* margarine
1	large onion, finely chopped
1	clove garlic, peeled and crushed
1 can	CAMPBELL's condensed Cream of Chicken Soup
350 ml	(*12 fl oz*) milk
	Pinch ground nutmeg
	Salt *and* ground black pepper
	Chopped fresh parsley for garnish

■ In large saucepan, place squash; add water to cover squash. Over high heat, heat to boiling. Reduce heat to low. Cover; simmer gently 10 minutes or until squash is tender. Drain. In covered blender or food processor, blend squash until smooth.

■ In same saucepan over moderate heat, in hot butter, gently fry onion and garlic until softened, stirring occasionally. Add puréed squash, soup, milk and nutmeg. Season to taste with salt and pepper. Heat to simmer. Reduce heat to low; simmer gently 5 minutes.

■ Stir in milk. Heat through, stirring occasionally. If necessary, thin to desired consistency with more milk or water. Heat through. Garnish with parsley, if liked.

Serves 4 to 5 as a starter.
Prep Time: 20 minutes
Cook Time: 35 minutes

1 Gently simmer squash in water until tender.

BUTTERNUT SQUASH BISQUE

2   Drain squash, then blend in food processor.

3   Add puréed squash to cooked onion and garlic mixture.

4   Stir in milk and mix well.

CREAMY CHICKEN-BROCCOLI SOUP

CREAMY CHICKEN-BROCCOLI SOUP

25 g	(*1 oz*) **butter** *or* **margarine**
75 g	(*3 oz*) **button mushrooms, wiped and sliced**
1	**small onion, chopped**
1	**small red** *or* **green pepper, de-seeded and cut into strips**
1	**clove garlic, peeled and crushed (optional)**
2.5 ml	(*½ tsp*) **dried basil**
1 can	**CAMPBELL'S condensed Cream of Chicken Soup**
300 ml	(*½ pt*) **chicken stock**
350 ml	(*12 fl oz*) **milk**
225 g	(*8 oz*) **roughly chopped, cooked chicken**
75 g	(*3 oz*) **broccoli florets**
	Pinch ground black pepper
	Pinch ground nutmeg

■ In large saucepan over moderate heat, in hot butter, gently fry mushrooms, onion, red pepper, garlic and basil until vegetables are tender, stirring occasionally.

■ Stir in soup and stock. Stir in milk, chicken, broccoli, pepper and nutmeg. Heat to simmer. Reduce heat to low. Cover; simmer gently 5 minutes or until broccoli is tender.

Serves 4 as a main dish.
Prep Time: 15 minutes
Cook Time: 20 minutes

TOMATO DILL SOUP

1 can	**CAMPBELL'S condensed Cream of Tomato Soup**
300 ml	(*½ pt*) **milk**
1.2 ml	(*¼ tsp*) **dried dill weed**
	Sour cream

In small saucepan, stir soup. Gradually add milk. Add dill. Over moderate heat, heat through, stirring occasionally. Serve with sour cream.

To microwave: In 1.5-Lt (*2-¾-pt*) microwave-proof dish, stir soup. Gradually add milk. Add dill. Cover; microwave on HIGH 6 minutes, stirring once during cooking. Serve with sour cream.

Serves 2 to 3 as a starter.
Prep Time: 5 minutes
Cook Time: 5 minutes

LENTIL CURRY SOUP

15 ml	(*1 tbsp*) **vegetable oil**
1	**small onion, finely chopped**
30 ml	(*2 tbsp*) **mild curry powder**
2 cans	**CAMPBELL'S condensed Lentil Soup**
450 ml	(*¾ pt*) **water**
100 g	(*4 oz*) **sultanas**
2	**hard-boiled eggs, shelled and chopped**

■ In large saucepan, over moderate heat, in hot oil, gently fry onion until softened. Stir in curry powder. Gently fry mixture 2 to 3 minutes, stirring constantly.

■ Stir in soup, water and sultanas. Heat to simmer. Reduce heat to low. Simmer gently 20 minutes, stirring regularly. Garnish with eggs just before serving.

Serves 4 as a main dish.
Prep Time: 10 minutes
Cook Time: 35 minutes

TOMATO BEEF STEW

225 g	**(*8 oz*) minced beef**
1 can	**CAMPBELL'S condensed Cream of Tomato Soup**
150 ml	**(*¼ pt*) water**
100 g	**(*4 oz*) frozen cut green beans**
50 g	**(*2 oz*) frozen sliced carrots**
5 ml	**(*1 tsp*) Worcestershire sauce**

■ In small saucepan over moderate heat, gently fry mince until well browned, stirring to separate meat. Spoon off fat.

■ Stir in soup and water. Add beans, carrots and Worcestershire sauce. Heat to simmering. Reduce heat to low. Simmer gently 20 minutes or until vegetables are tender, stirring occasionally.

Garden Vegetable Beef Stew: Prepare Tomato Beef Stew as directed above, *except* substitute 175 g (*6 oz*) *frozen mixed vegetables* for the green beans and carrots. Add vegetables as directed above.

Serves 2 as a main dish.
Prep Time: 5 minutes
Cook Time: 25 minutes

SPEEDY SPICY CHILLI

450 g	(*1 lb*) minced beef
1	medium onion, chopped
1	clove garlic, peeled and crushed
10 ml	(*2 tsp*) hot chilli powder
1 can (450 g)	(*16 oz*) baked beans with bacon in tomato sauce
1 can	CAMPBELL'S condensed Cream of Tomato Soup
150 ml	(*¾ pt*) water
	Sliced spring onions *and* sour cream for garnish

■ In large frying pan over moderate-high heat, gently fry mince, onion, garlic and chilli powder until meat is well browned and onion is softened, stirring to separate meat. Spoon off fat.

■ Add beans, soup and water. Heat to simmer. Reduce heat to low. Simmer gently 10 minutes, stirring occasionally. Garnish with onion and sour cream, if liked.

TIP: Serve with bowls of chopped tomato, grated cheese, sliced spring onions and sour cream to add pizzazz to this extra-fast chilli.

Serves 4 as a main dish.
Prep Time: 10 minutes
Cook Time: 20 minutes

CINCINNATI CHILLI

450 g	(*1 lb*) minced beef
1	medium green pepper, de-seeded and chopped
1	small onion, chopped
15 to 30 ml	(*1 to 2 tbsp*) hot chilli powder
2	cloves garlic, peeled and crushed
2 cans	CAMPBELL'S condensed Cream of Tomato Soup
1 can (439 g)	(*15½ oz*) red kidney beans, undrained
15 ml	(*1 tbsp*) malt vinegar
1.2 ml	(*¼ tsp*) ground cinnamon
	Freshly cooked spaghetti
	Grated Cheddar cheese for garnish

■ In large saucepan over moderate heat, gently fry mince, green pepper, onion, chilli powder and garlic until meat is well browned and onion is softened, stirring to separate meat. Spoon off fat.

■ Stir in soup, undrained beans, vinegar and cinnamon. Heat to simmer. Reduce heat to low. Simmer gently 15 minutes, stirring occasionally.

■ Serve over spaghetti. Sprinkle with cheese, if liked.

Serves 4 to 5 as a main dish.
Prep Time: 15 minutes
Cook Time: 30 minutes

SPEEDY SPICY CHILLI (top)
CINCINNATI CHILLI (bottom)

COUNTRY CHICKEN STEW

15 ml	(*1 tbsp*) vegetable oil
2	rindless rashers streaky bacon
1	medium onion, sliced into rings
5 ml	(*1 tsp*) dried oregano
1 can	CAMPBELL'S condensed Cream of Chicken Soup
300 ml	(*1/2 pt*) water
4	medium potatoes, peeled and cut into chunks
2	medium carrots, peeled and diagonally sliced
100 g	(*4 oz*) frozen cut green beans
225 g	(*8 oz*) cubed, cooked chicken
30 ml	(*2 tbsp*) chopped fresh parsley

■ In large frying pan over moderate heat, in hot oil, gently fry bacon until crisp. Transfer to absorbent kitchen paper to drain, reserving fat; set aside. Crumble bacon; set aside.

■ In hot fat, gently fry onion and oregano until onion is softened.

■ Stir in soup, water, potatoes and carrots; heat to simmer, stirring occasionally. Reduce heat to low. Cover; simmer gently 15 minutes, stirring occasionally.

■ Stir in beans. Cover; simmer gently 10 minutes. Stir in chicken; heat through. Sprinkle with reserved bacon and parsley.

Serves 4 as a main dish.
Prep Time: 15 minutes
Cook Time: 40 minutes

1 Gently fry bacon until crisp.

2 Gently fry onion and oregano in hot fat.

COUNTRY CHICKEN STEW

3 Stir in soup, water, potatoes and carrots. Cover; simmer gently 15 minutes.

4 Stir in beans. Cover; simmer gently 10 minutes.

CELERY FISH CHOWDER

15 g	(*½ oz*) butter *or* margarine
100 g	(*4 oz*) sliced, trimmed celery
1	medium onion, chopped
2	cloves garlic, peeled and crushed
45 ml	(*3 tbsp*) dry white wine *or* milk
2 cans	CAMPBELL'S condensed Cream of Celery Soup
600 ml	(*1 pt*) milk
450 g	(*1 lb*) firm white fish fillets, cut into 2.5-cm (*1-in*) cubes
½	small red pepper, de-seeded and finely diced (optional)
	Generous pinch cayenne pepper (optional)

■ In large saucepan over moderate heat, in hot butter, gently fry celery, onion and garlic until softened, stirring regularly.

■ Add wine; simmer gently 2 minutes. Stir in soup. Gradually stir in milk. Add fish, red pepper and cayenne. Heat to simmer. Reduce heat to low. Cover; simmer gently 5 minutes or until fish flakes easily when tested with fork.

TIP: Use haddock, halibut or cod in this vegetable chowder.

Serves 4 as a main dish.
Prep Time: 15 minutes
Cook Time: 20 minutes

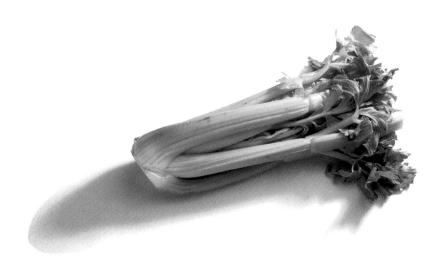

CELERY FISH CHOWDER

SMOKED TURKEY BEAN SOUP

15 ml	(*1 tbsp*) vegetable oil
1	medium onion, chopped
2	cloves garlic, peeled and crushed
1 can	CAMPBELL'S condensed Cream of Chicken Soup
1 can (430 g)	(*15 oz*) white cannellini beans, drained
300 ml	(*½ pt*) water
100 g	(*4 oz*) smoked turkey breast, cut into 1-cm (*½-in*) pieces
5 ml	(*1 tsp*) paprika
15 ml	(*1 tbsp*) chopped fresh parsley (optional)

■ In medium saucepan over moderate heat, in hot oil, gently fry onion and garlic until softened, stirring occasionally.

■ Stir in soup, beans, water, turkey and paprika. Heat to simmer. Reduce heat to low. Simmer gently 5 minutes. Stir in parsley. Garnish with fresh *parsley sprig*, if liked.

TIP: You can substitute leftover roast turkey or baked ham for the smoked turkey.

Serves 2 to 3 as a main dish.
Prep Time: 10 minutes
Cook Time: 15 minutes

QUICK GAZPACHO

1 can	**CAMPBELL'S condensed Cream of Tomato Soup**
300 ml	**(*½ pt*) water**
½	**cucumber, peeled and chopped**
1	**celery stick, trimmed and chopped**
1	**small carrot, peeled and chopped**
2	**spring onions, trimmed and sliced**
15 ml	**(*1 tbsp*) lemon juice**
	Celery leaves for garnish

■ In large bowl, stir soup. Gradually stir in water until smooth.

■ Add cucumber, celery, carrot, onions and lemon juice. Cover and refrigerate at least 2 hours before serving. Garnish with celery leaves, if liked.

Serves 2 to 3 as a starter.
Prep Time: 15 minutes
Chill Time: 2 hours

TACO SOUP

1 can	**CAMPBELL'S condensed Cream of Tomato Soup**
300 ml	**(1/2 pt) water**
45 ml	**(3 tbsp) salsa or taco sauce**
	Crumbled tortilla chips
	Grated Cheddar cheese
	Sliced spring onions
	Sour cream

■ In small saucepan, combine soup, water and salsa. Over moderate heat, heat through, stirring occasionally.

■ Sprinkle *each* serving with tortilla chips, Cheddar cheese and spring onions; top with a spoonful of sour cream.

Serves 2 as a starter.
Prep Time: 5 minutes
Cook Time: 5 minutes

SAUSAGE SWEETCORN CHOWDER

225 g	(*8 oz*) pork sausagemeat
4	spring onions, trimmed and sliced
1 can	CAMPBELL'S condensed Cream of Chicken Soup
300 ml	(*½ pt*) milk
1 can (198 g)	(*7 oz*) sweetcorn, undrained
50 g	(*2 oz*) Emmental cheese, grated
1.2 ml	(*¼ tsp*) Tabasco sauce

■ In large saucepan over moderate heat, gently fry sausagemeat until browned, stirring to separate meat. Spoon off fat.

■ Add spring onions. Gently fry 1 minute, stirring occasionally.

■ Stir in soup, milk, sweetcorn, Emmental cheese and Tabasco sauce. Heat through, stirring occasionally.

Serves 4 as a starter.
Prep Time: 10 minutes
Cook Time: 15 minutes

SOUTHERN-STYLE BRUNSWICK STEW

2	**rindless rashers streaky bacon**
1	**small onion, chopped**
1 can	**CAMPBELL'S condensed Cream of Tomato Soup**
300 ml	**(1/2 pt) water**
5 ml	**(1 tsp) Worcestershire sauce**
	Generous pinch ground black pepper
275 g	**(10 oz) frozen broad beans**
275 g	**(10 oz) frozen sweetcorn**
275 g	**(10 oz) cubed, cooked chicken**

■ In large saucepan over low heat, gently fry bacon until crisp. Transfer to absorbent kitchen paper to drain, reserving *15 ml (1 tbsp)* fat in pan. Crumble bacon; set aside.

■ Over moderate heat, in hot fat, gently fry onion until softened, stirring occasionally.

■ Stir in soup, water, Worcestershire sauce and pepper. Heat to simmer. Add broad beans and sweetcorn. Return to simmer. Stir to separate vegetables. Reduce heat to low. Cover; simmer gently 20 minutes, stirring occasionally.

■ Stir in chicken and reserved bacon; heat through.

Serves 4 as a main dish.
Prep Time: 15 minutes
Cook Time: 30 minutes

1 Gently fry onion until softened.

2 Stir in soup, water, Worcestershire sauce and pepper.

3 Add vegetables. Mix well.

SOUTHERN-STYLE BRUNSWICK STEW

4 Add chicken and bacon.

SPICY BEAN SOUP

15 ml	(*1 tbsp*) vegetable oil
1	small green pepper, de-seeded and chopped
1	small onion, chopped
1 can	CAMPBELL'S condensed Cream of Tomato Soup
1 can (440 g)	(*15½ oz*) chick peas, drained
1 can (440 g)	(*15½ oz*) red kidney beans *or* black beans, drained
300 ml	(*½ pt*) water
5 ml	(*1 tsp*) Worcestershire sauce
1.2 ml	(*¼ tsp*) Tabasco sauce
100 g	(*4 oz*) Cheddar cheese, grated

■ In large saucepan over moderate heat, in hot oil, gently fry green pepper and onion 5 minutes or until softened, stirring occasionally.

■ Stir in soup, chick peas, beans, water, Worcestershire and Tabasco sauce. Heat to simmer, stirring occasionally. Reduce heat to low. Cover; simmer gently 5 minutes. Sprinkle with Cheddar cheese.

TIP: Serve this hearty vegetable soup with tortilla chips.

Serves 4 as a starter.
Prep Time: 10 minutes
Cook Time: 20 minutes

SPICY BEAN SOUP

CHICKEN KORMA

30 ml	(*2 tbsp*) vegetable oil
450 g	(*1 lb*) boneless chicken breasts *or* thighs, skinned and cut into 4-cm (*1½-in*) cubes
1	medium onion, thinly sliced
1 can	CAMPBELL'S condensed Cream of Chicken Soup
300 ml	(*½ pt*) water *or* milk
45 to 60 ml	(*3 to 4 tbsp*) mild curry paste
	Salt *and* ground black pepper
	Freshly cooked rice

■ In large frying pan over moderate-high heat, in hot oil, gently fry chicken and onion 5 minutes or until chicken is lightly browned and onion is softened, stirring regularly.

■ Stir in soup, water and curry paste. Heat to simmer. Reduce heat to low. Simmer gently 30 minutes or until chicken is tender and flavours are blended, stirring occasionally. Season to taste with salt and pepper. Serve with rice.

TIP: If liked, stir in 25 g (*1 oz*) roughly chopped creamed coconut or 25 g (*1 oz*) ground almonds 5 minutes before end of cooking time. Sprinkle with additional flaked or ground almonds before serving.

Serves 4.
Prep Time: 10 minutes
Cook Time: 35 minutes

CHICKEN TIKKA MASALA

450 g	(*1 lb*) boneless chicken breasts *or* thighs, skinned and cut into 4-cm (*1½-in*) cubes
30 ml	(*2 tbsp*) tikka seasoning mix
15 ml	(*1 tbsp*) vegetable oil
1 can	CAMPBELL'S condensed Cream of Tomato Soup
200 ml	(*7 fl oz*) milk

■ In medium bowl, toss chicken and seasoning mix until evenly coated.

■ In large saucepan over moderate heat, in hot oil, gently fry chicken 5 minutes or until browned, stirring regularly.

■ Stir soup and milk into saucepan. Heat to simmer. Reduce heat to low. Simmer gently 25 minutes or until chicken is tender, stirring occasionally.

Serves 4.
Prep Time: 10 minutes
Cook Time: 30 minutes

CHICKEN IN SPICY PEANUT SAUCE

4	boneless chicken breasts, skinned
30 ml	(*2 tbsp*) vegetable oil
1 can	**CAMPBELL'S condensed Cream of Chicken Soup**
45 ml	(*3 tbsp*) crunchy peanut butter
150 ml	(*¼ pt*) water
2	spring onions, trimmed and sliced
2.5 ml	(*½ tsp*) hot chilli powder
1.2 ml	(*¼ tsp*) cayenne pepper

■ Place chicken breasts between 2 sheets of plastic wrap. With flat edge of meat mallet or rolling pin, pound to 5-mm (*¼-in*) thickness.

■ In large frying pan over moderate heat, in hot oil, gently fry chicken 10 minutes or until browned on both sides. Remove chicken from frying pan. Spoon off fat.

■ Add soup, peanut butter, water, spring onions, chilli powder and cayenne pepper to frying pan; stir until smooth. Heat to simmer. Return chicken to frying pan. Reduce heat to low. Cover; simmer gently 10 minutes or until chicken is tender, stirring occasionally.

Serves 4.
Prep Time: 15 minutes
Cook Time: 35 minutes

TURKEY WITH APPLE-PECAN STUFFING

50 g	(*2 oz*) **butter** *or* **margarine**
100 g	(*4 oz*) **chopped, trimmed celery**
1	**medium onion, chopped**
2 cans	**CAMPBELL'S condensed Consommé**
2 pkt (170 g each)	(*6 oz each*) **sage and onion stuffing mix**
2	**medium eating apples, quartered, cored and chopped**
100 g	(*4 oz*) **shelled pecan nuts** *or* **walnuts, toasted and chopped**
6- to 7-kg	(*14- to 16-lb*) **ready-to-stuff turkey, cleaned**
	Apple slices for garnish

■ *To prepare stuffing:* In large saucepan over moderate heat, in hot butter, gently fry celery and onion until softened. Add consommé; heat to simmer. Remove from heat. Add stuffing mix, apples and pecans; toss to mix well.

■ Spoon stuffing mixture lightly into turkey neck and body cavities. Fold skin over stuffing; secure with skewers. Tie legs. On rack in roasting pan, place turkey breast-side up. (Insert meat thermometer into thickest part of turkey between breast and thigh, not touching bone.)

■ Cover with buttered foil. Roast at 180 °C (*350 °F, gas mark 4*) for 20 minutes to the 450 g (*1 lb*) or until juices run clear and drumstick moves easily when twisted. Baste turkey occasionally with drippings. Remove foil 30 minutes before end of roasting. [Internal temperature should reach 82 °C (*180 °F*).] Garnish with apple, if liked.

To prepare stuffing separately: Prepare stuffing as directed above. Spoon stuffing mixture into greased shallow ovenproof dish. Cover; bake at 190 °C (*375 °F, gas mark 5*) for 30 minutes or until hot.

Serves 14 to 16.
Prep Time: 25 minutes
Cook Time: 4 to 5 hours

1 Gently fry celery and onion until softened.

2 After consommé has been brought to a simmer, remove pan from heat. Add stuffing mix, apples and pecans.

TURKEY WITH APPLE-PECAN STUFFING

3 Spoon stuffing into urkey neck and body cavities.

4 Fold skin over stuffing; secure with skewers.

GINGER CHICKEN STIR-FRY

45 ml	(*3 tbsp*) vegetable oil
450 g	(*1 lb*) boneless chicken breasts *or* thighs, skinned, cut into strips
350 g	(*12 oz*) fresh prepared vegetables (e.g. broccoli, red pepper, green beans, cauliflower, red onion *or* mangetout)
1	clove garlic, peeled and crushed
1 can	CAMPBELL'S condensed Consommé
30 ml	(*2 tbsp*) cornflour
15 ml	(*1 tbsp*) light soy sauce
2.5 ml	(*½ tsp*) ground ginger
	Freshly cooked noodles *or* rice
	Toasted flaked almonds

■ In large frying pan or wok over moderate-high heat, in *30 ml (2 tbsp)* hot oil, stir-fry chicken until browned. Remove; set aside.

■ In same frying pan in remaining *15 ml (1 tbsp)* oil, stir-fry vegetables and garlic until tender-crisp.

■ Meanwhile, in bowl, combine consommé, cornflour, soy sauce and ginger until smooth. Add to frying pan along with reserved chicken. Simmer gently until mixture thickens, stirring regularly. Serve over noodles. Sprinkle with toasted almonds.

TIP: When stir-frying, it's easier to lift and turn the meat and vegetables if you use a long-handled spoon or spatula.

TIP: Chinese rice noodles are available in the specialty sections of most supermarkets. The *uncooked* noodles can either be cooked in simmering water, drained and used as traditional noodles, or fried in hot oil until crispy.

Serves 4.
Prep Time: 20 minutes
Cook Time: 15 minutes

GINGER CHICKEN STIR-FRY

COUNTRY-STYLE SMOTHERED CHICKEN

2	**rindless rashers bacon**
8	**chicken parts (e.g. thighs and drumsticks)**
1 can	**CAMPBELL'S condensed Cream of Mushroom Soup**
1	**clove garlic, peeled and crushed**
5 ml	**(*1 tsp*) dried basil**
1	**medium onion, sliced**
	Freshly cooked rice
	Fresh basil for garnish

■ In large frying pan over moderate heat, gently fry bacon until crisp. Transfer to absorbent kitchen paper to drain, reserving fat in pan. Crumble bacon; set aside.

■ Over moderate heat, in hot fat, gently fry chicken 10 minutes or until browned on all sides. Spoon off fat.

■ Stir soup, garlic and basil into frying pan. Heat to simmer. Reduce heat to low. Cover; simmer gently 20 minutes.

■ Add onion. Cover; simmer gently 15 to 20 minutes more or until chicken is no longer pink and juices run clear, stirring occasionally. Serve over rice. Sprinkle with reserved bacon. Garnish with basil, if liked.

Serves 4.
Prep Time: 10 minutes
Cook Time: 50 to 55 minutes

CHICKEN PASTA PARMESAN

30 ml	(*2 tbsp*) **vegetable oil**
450 g	(*1 lb*) **boneless chicken breasts, skinned and cut into 2.5-cm (*1-in*) cubes**
½	**small onion, chopped**
1 can	**CAMPBELL'S condensed Cream of Chicken Soup**
30 ml	(*2 tbsp*) **milk**
15 ml	(*1 tbsp*) **dry sherry (optional)**
100 g	(*4 oz*) **broccoli florets**
75 g	(*3 oz*) **button mushrooms, wiped and sliced**
40 g	(*1½ oz*) **grated Parmesan cheese**
	Freshly cooked spaghetti

■ In large frying pan over moderate heat, in hot oil, gently fry chicken and onion until chicken is browned and onion is softened.

■ Stir in soup, milk and sherry. Add broccoli, mushrooms and Parmesan cheese. Heat to simmer. Reduce heat to low. Cover; simmer gently 15 minutes or until chicken is tender, stirring occasionally.

■ Serve over spaghetti. Serve with additional grated *Parmesan cheese*, if liked.

TIP: If liked, substitute 1 medium thinly sliced, de-seeded green or red pepper, for the broccoli.

Serves 4.
Prep Time: 15 minutes
Cook Time: 25 minutes

CHICKEN MOZZARELLA

4	**boneless chicken breasts, skinned**
30 ml	(*2 tbsp*) **plain flour**
5 ml	(*1 tsp*) **dried basil**
15 ml	(*1 tbsp*) **vegetable oil**
1 can	**CAMPBELL'S condensed Cream of Tomato Soup**
30 ml	(*2 tbsp*) **water**
4	**slices mozzarella cheese**
	Chopped green pepper (optional)

■ Place chicken breasts between 2 sheets of plastic wrap. With flat side of meat mallet or rolling pin, pound chicken to 5-mm (*¼-in*) thickness. On plate, combine flour and basil. Coat chicken lightly with flour mixture.

■ In large frying pan over moderate-high heat, in hot oil, gently fry chicken 10 minutes or until browned on both sides.

■ Stir in soup and water, stirring to loosen browned bits. Heat to simmer. Reduce heat to low. Simmer gently 10 minutes or until chicken is tender.

■ Top each chicken breast with a mozzarella cheese slice and sprinkle with green pepper. Heat until cheese melts.

Serves 4.
Prep Time: 15 minutes
Cook Time: 25 minutes

1 Place chicken between 2 sheets of plastic wrap.

2 Pound the chicken using a meat mallet.

3 Gently fry chicken in a frying pan until browned on both sides.

4 Stir soup and water into frying pan. Stir to loosen browned bits.

CHICKEN MOZZARELLA

Turkey-Vegetable Pot Pie

450 g	(*1 lb*) frozen mixed vegetables (e.g. broccoli, cauliflower and carrots)
25 g	(*1 oz*) butter *or* margarine
1	small onion, chopped
75 g	(*3 oz*) sliced, trimmed celery
2.5 ml	(*½ tsp*) dried thyme
2 cans	CAMPBELL'S condensed Cream of Chicken & Mushroom Soup
300 ml	(*½ pt*) milk
350 g	(*12 oz*) diced, cooked turkey *or* chicken
1.2 ml	(*¼ tsp*) ground black pepper
1 pkt (225 g)	(*8 oz*) frozen *or* refrigerated puff pastry (thawed if frozen)
	Beaten egg to glaze

■ Preheat oven to 190 °C (*375 °F, gas mark 5*). Cook vegetables according to packet directions; drain.

■ Meanwhile, in medium saucepan over moderate heat, in hot butter, gently fry onion, celery and thyme until onion is softened, stirring occasionally. Stir in soup and milk.

■ In 1.75-Lt (*3-pt*) pie dish, combine cooked vegetables, turkey and pepper. Add soup mixture, stirring gently to mix.

■ On lightly floured surface, roll pastry into a 30- by 23-cm (*12- by 9-in*) rectangle. Cut pastry lengthwise into 8 strips, each about 2.5 cm (*1 in*) wide. Arrange strips over turkey mixture to form a lattice, cutting strips as necessary to fit. Press ends of strips to pie dish. Brush pastry with beaten egg.

■ Bake 40 minutes or until golden brown.

Serves 6.
Prep Time: 30 minutes
Cook Time: 50 minutes

TURKEY-VEGETABLE POT PIE

*S*PANISH CHICKEN AND RICE

30 ml	(*2 tbsp*) **vegetable oil**
8	**chicken parts (e.g. thighs and drumsticks)**
1 can	**CAMPBELL'S condensed Cream of Chicken Soup**
1	**medium green pepper, de-seeded and diced**
1 can (220 g)	(*8 oz*) **chopped tomatoes, drained**
100 g	(*4 oz*) *uncooked* **long-grain rice**
3	**cloves garlic, peeled and crushed**
2.5 ml	(*¹/₂ tsp*) **Tabasco sauce**
	Fresh parsley sprigs for garnish

■ In large frying pan over moderate-high heat, in hot oil, gently fry chicken 10 minutes or until browned on all sides. Remove chicken; set aside. Spoon off fat.

■ Stir soup, green pepper, tomatoes, rice, garlic and Tabasco sauce into frying pan. Heat to simmer. Reduce heat to low. Return chicken to frying pan. Simmer gently 35 minutes or until liquid is absorbed and chicken is no longer pink and juices run clear, stirring occasionally.

■ To serve, spoon some rice mixture on each plate and top with chicken. Garnish with parsley, if liked.

TIP: When you shop, select chicken that is plump; that's a good indication it will be moist and meaty. Also look for poultry with skin that is white to deep yellow with no bruises or discolouration.

Serves 4.
Prep Time: 15 minutes
Cook Time: 50 minutes

$\mathcal{G}$OLDEN CHICKEN GRILL

1 can	**CAMPBELL'S condensed Creamy Vegetable Soup**
150 ml	**(¼ pt) milk**
450 g	**(1 lb) boneless chicken breasts or thighs, skinned, cut into 2.5-cm (1-in) cubes**
75 g	**(3 oz) fresh white or brown breadcrumbs**
50 g	**(2 oz) Cheddar cheese, grated**

■ In large saucepan, combine soup and milk. Stir in chicken. Over moderate heat, simmer gently 20 minutes or until chicken is tender, stirring occasionally. Spoon into warmed 1.15-Lt (*2-pt*) ovenproof dish.

■ In small bowl, combine breadcrumbs and Cheddar cheese; sprinkle over chicken mixture. Place under preheated hot grill 5 minutes or until topping is golden brown.

TIP: To warm dish, place under hot running water then dry.

Serves 4.
Prep Time: 10 minutes
Cook Time: 30 minutes

$\mathcal{C}$HINESE CHICKEN

1 can	**CAMPBELL'S condensed Cream of Chicken Soup**
30 ml	**(2 tbsp) caster sugar**
30 ml	**(2 tbsp) malt or white wine vinegar**
30 ml	**(2 tbsp) light soy sauce**
30 ml	**(2 tbsp) tomato ketchup**
2.5 ml	**(½ tsp) hot chilli powder**
15 ml	**(1 tbsp) vegetable oil**
450 g	**(1 lb) boneless chicken breasts, skinned and cut into 1-cm (½-in) thin strips**
4	**spring onions, trimmed and sliced**
1	**small red or green pepper, de-seeded and sliced**
100 g	**(4 oz) button mushrooms, wiped and sliced**
75 g	**(3 oz) broccoli florets**
	Freshly cooked rice

■ In medium bowl, combine soup, sugar, vinegar, soy sauce, ketchup and chilli powder. Set aside.

■ In large frying pan or wok over moderate-high heat, in hot oil, stir-fry chicken 3 minutes or until lightly browned. Add spring onions, red pepper, mushrooms and broccoli. Stir-fry 2 minutes.

■ Stir soup mixture into frying pan. Heat to simmer. Simmer 2 minutes or until chicken is tender and mixture is hot, stirring occasionally. Serve with rice.

Serves 4 to 5.
Prep Time: 10 minutes
Cook Time: 10 minutes

CHICKEN ORIENTAL

15 ml	(*1 tbsp*) **vegetable oil**
450 g	(*1 lb*) **boneless chicken breasts** *or* **thighs, skinned and cut into strips**
1	**small red onion, cut into 2.5-cm** (*1-in*) **pieces**
1	**medium green** *or* **red pepper, de-seeded and cut into 2.5-cm** (*1-in*) **squares**
1 can	**CAMPBELL'S condensed Cream of Chicken Soup**
45 ml	(*3 tbsp*) **water**
30 ml	(*2 tbsp*) **soy sauce**
	Freshly cooked rice
	Sliced spring onions for garnish
	Soy sauce

■ In large frying pan over moderate-high heat, in hot oil, gently fry chicken, *half* at a time, until browned. Remove; set aside. Repeat with remaining chicken.

■ Return chicken to frying pan. Add red onion and green pepper. Gently fry 5 minutes or until chicken is tender.

■ Stir in soup, water and soy sauce. Heat to simmer. Reduce heat to low. Simmer gently 5 minutes or until chicken is tender, stirring occasionally.

■ Serve chicken mixture over rice. Garnish with spring onions and serve with additional soy sauce, if liked.

Serves 4.
Prep Time: 15 minutes
Cook Time: 25 to 30 minutes

1 Gently fry chicken, *half* at a time, until browned.

2 Return all browned chicken to frying pan.

3 Add red onion and green pepper. Gently fry 5 minutes.

CHICKEN ORIENTAL

4 Stir in soup, water and soy sauce. Heat mixture to simmer.

SPEEDY CHICKEN CASSEROLE

8	chicken parts (e.g. thighs and drumsticks)
1 can	CAMPBELL'S condensed Cream of Chicken *or* Cream of Mushroom Soup
150 ml	(1/4 pt) water
450 g	(1 lb) frozen mixed vegetables (e.g. peas, sweetcorn, green beans and carrots)

- Preheat oven to 200 °C (*400 °F, gas mark 6*).

- Arrange chicken in shallow 2-Lt (*3 1/2-pt*) ovenproof dish. Bake 15 minutes or until lightly browned. Spoon off fat.

- In large bowl, combine soup and water. Stir in vegetables. Spoon over chicken. Bake 30 minutes more or until chicken is no longer pink and juices run clear, stirring occasionally.

Serves 4.
Prep Time: 5 minutes
Cook Time: 45 minutes

CHICKEN SUPREME

4	boneless chicken breasts, skinned
15 g	(1/2 oz) plain flour seasoned with salt *and* ground black pepper
30 ml	(2 tbsp) vegetable oil
1 can	CAMPBELL'S condensed Cream of Mushroom, Cream of Chicken, Chicken & Mushroom, Ham & Cheese *or* Mushroom & Peppers Soup
300 ml	(1/2 pt) milk
	Salt *and* ground black pepper
	Freshly cooked rice *or* new potatoes

- On plate, coat chicken with seasoned flour.

- In large frying pan over moderate-high heat, in hot oil, gently fry chicken 10 minutes or until lightly browned on both sides. Spoon off fat.

- In small bowl, combine soup and milk. Stir into frying pan. Heat to simmer. Reduce heat to low. Simmer gently 15 to 20 minutes or until chicken is tender, stirring occasionally. Season to taste with salt and pepper. Serve with rice or potatoes.

TIP: If liked, add 50 g (*2 oz*) frozen peas to chicken mixture 5 minutes before end of cooking time.

Turkey Supreme: Prepare Chicken Supreme as directed above, *except* substitute 450 g (*1 lb*) boneless *turkey breasts,* cut into 1-cm (*1/2-in*) strips, for the chicken. Reduce simmering time for the turkey mixture 5 minutes.

Serves 4.
Prep Time: 5 minutes
Cook Time: 25 to 30 minutes

CREAMY CHICKEN LASAGNE

2 cans	**CAMPBELL'S condensed Ham & Cheese Soup**
150 ml	**(¼ pt) milk**
350 g	**(12 oz) diced, cooked chicken**
100 g	**(4 oz) fresh prepared spinach, shredded**
	Salt *and* ground black pepper
75 to 100 g	**(3 to 4 oz) no pre-cook dried lasagne sheets**
100 g	**(4 oz) Cheddar cheese, grated**

■ Preheat oven to 200 °C (*400°F, gas mark 6*).

■ In large bowl, combine soup and milk. Stir in chicken and spinach. Season to taste with salt and pepper. Spoon ⅓ of soup mixture into 1.75-Lt (*3-pt*) rectangular ovenproof dish. Top with ½ of lasagne sheets. Repeat layers, ending with soup mixture. Sprinkle with Cheddar cheese.

■ Bake 30 minutes or until golden brown and bubbling.

Serves 4 to 5.
Prep Time: 20 minutes
Cook Time: 30 minutes

CREAMY CHICKEN WITH MUSHROOMS

15 ml	**(1 tbsp) vegetable oil**
1	**small onion, thinly sliced**
1	**clove garlic, peeled and crushed (optional)**
4	**boneless chicken breasts, skinned**
1 can	**CAMPBELL'S condensed Cream of Chicken *or* Cream of Mushroom Soup**
300 ml	**(½ pt) milk**
30 to 45 ml	**(2 to 3 tbsp) dry sherry *or* water**
100 g	**(4 oz) button mushrooms, wiped and sliced**
	Salt *and* ground black pepper
	Fresh basil leaves, fresh mushrooms *and* lemon slices for garnish

■ In large frying pan over moderate heat, in hot oil, gently fry onion and garlic until softened. Add chicken; gently fry until lightly browned on both sides. Spoon off fat.

■ In medium bowl, combine soup, milk, sherry and mushrooms; stir into frying pan. Heat to simmer. Reduce heat to low. Simmer gently 15 to 20 minutes or until chicken is tender, stirring occasionally. Season to taste with salt and pepper. Garnish with basil, mushrooms and lemon slices, if liked.

TIP: Prepare Creamy Chicken with Mushrooms as directed above, *except* substitute 8 chicken parts (e.g. thighs and drumsticks) for the boneless chicken breasts. After adding soup mixture, gently simmer 30 minutes or until chicken is no longer pink and juices run clear.

Serves 4.
Prep Time: 10 minutes
Cook Time: 30 to 35 minutes

CHICKEN AND MUSHROOM PIE

1 can	**CAMPBELL'S condensed Cream of Chicken, Cream of Mushroom or Ham & Cheese Soup**
150 ml	**(¼ pt) milk**
350 g	**(12 oz) cubed, cooked chicken**
100 g	**(4 oz) button mushrooms, wiped and halved**
75 g	**(3 oz) frozen peas**
2.5 ml	**(½ tsp) dried mixed herbs**
	Salt and ground black pepper
1 pkt (225 g)	**(8 oz) frozen or refrigerated puff pastry, (thawed if frozen)**
	Milk to brush and glaze

■ Preheat oven to 200 °C (*400 °F, gas mark 6*).

■ In 1.15-Lt (*2-pt*) pie dish, combine soup and milk. Stir in chicken, mushrooms, peas and herbs. Season to taste with salt and pepper.

■ Brush rim of dish with milk. On lightly floured surface, roll pastry slightly larger than diameter of dish. Place over filling.

■ Press firmly to seal. Trim and flute edge. Brush pastry with additional milk to glaze. With small knife, make a small hole in middle of pastry. Bake 35 to 40 minutes or until pastry is puffed and golden brown.

Serves 4.
Prep Time: 20 to 25 minutes
Cook Time: 35 to 40 minutes

QUICK CHICKEN CHEESE CASSEROLE

1 can	**CAMPBELL'S condensed Ham & Cheese Soup**
200 ml	**(7 fl oz) milk**
4	**boneless chicken breasts, skinned**
75 g	**(3 oz) Cheddar cheese, finely grated**
50 g	**(2 oz) fresh white or brown breadcrumbs**

■ Preheat oven to 200 °C (*400 °F, gas mark 6*).

■ In small bowl, combine soup and milk. Arrange chicken breasts in shallow 1.4-Lt (*2½-pt*) ovenproof dish. Pour soup mixture over.

■ In small bowl, combine Cheddar cheese and breadcrumbs. Sprinkle over chicken. Bake 35 to 40 minutes or until chicken is tender and topping is golden brown.

Serves 4.
Prep Time: 10 minutes
Cook Time: 35 to 40 minutes

CHICKEN CASSEROLE

1 can	**CAMPBELL'S condensed Chicken & Mushroom, Cream of Chicken *or* Cream of Mushroom Soup**
150 ml	**(*¼ pt*) water *or* dry white wine**
100 g	**(*4 oz*) button mushrooms, wiped and halved**
15 ml	**(*1 tbsp*) vegetable oil**
8	**chicken parts (e.g. thighs and drumsticks)**
1	**medium onion, finely chopped**

■ Preheat oven to 200 °C (*400 °F, gas mark 6*). In 2-Lt (*3½-pt*) casserole dish, combine soup, water and mushrooms. Set aside.

■ In large frying pan over moderate heat, in hot oil, gently fry chicken and onion 10 minutes or until chicken is lightly browned on all sides and onion is softened. With slotted spoon, remove chicken and place in casserole, turning chicken pieces to coat with soup mixture. Cover.

■ Bake 35 minutes or until chicken is no longer pink and juices run clear, stirring after 20 minutes.

TIP: If liked, substitute 4 boneless chicken breasts, skinned, for the chicken thighs and drumsticks. Reduce baking time to 25 minutes or until chicken is tender, stirring after 15 minutes.

Serves 4.
Prep Time: 20 minutes
Cook Time: 45 minutes

GOLDEN CRUMBED CHICKEN

4	**boneless chicken breasts, skinned**
1	**(size 3) egg, lightly beaten**
75 to 100 g	**(*3 to 4 oz*) dried golden breadcrumbs**
45 to 60 ml	**(*3 to 4 tbsp*) vegetable oil**
1 can	**CAMPBELL'S condensed Chicken & Mushroom, Cream of Chicken, Ham & Cheese *or* Cream of Mushroom Soup**
200 ml	**(*7 fl oz*) milk**
	Salt *and* ground black pepper

■ Dip each chicken breast in egg and coat evenly in breadcrumbs.

■ In large frying pan over moderate heat, in hot oil, gently fry chicken 15 to 20 minutes or until browned on both sides and tender. Transfer chicken to absorbent kitchen paper to drain. Set aside; keep warm. Spoon off fat.

■ Stir soup and milk into same frying pan. Heat through, stirring regularly. Season to taste with salt and pepper. Serve over chicken.

Serves 4.
Prep Time: 10 minutes
Cook Time: 20 to 25 minutes

$\mathcal{B}$EEF STIR-FRY

30 ml	(*2 tbsp*) vegetable oil
450 g	(*1 lb*) rump steak, thinly sliced
225 g	(*8 oz*) cabbage, coarsely chopped
100 g	(*4 oz*) courgettes, trimmed and cut into 5-cm (*2-in*) matchstick-thin strips
1 can	CAMPBELL'S condensed Consommé
45 ml	(*3 tbsp*) dry sherry
30 ml	(*2 tbsp*) light soy sauce
30 ml	(*2 tbsp*) cornflour
150 ml	(*¼ pt*) water
100 g	(*4 oz*) cherry tomatoes, halved
	Freshly cooked rice

■ In large frying pan over high heat, in hot oil, gently fry beef, *half* at a time, until steak just changes colour, stirring regularly. Transfer to bowl.

■ Add cabbage and courgettes to frying pan. Over high heat, gently fry 1 minute, stirring regularly. Stir in consommé, sherry and soy sauce. Heat to simmer.

■ Meanwhile, in bowl, stir together cornflour and water until smooth. Gradually stir into consommé mixture. Simmer gently until thickened, stirring regularly. Add cooked steak and cherry tomatoes. Simmer 2 minutes more or until heated through, stirring regularly. Serve over rice.

Serves 4.
Prep Time: 15 minutes
Cook Time: 15 to 20 minutes

LASAGNE

1 can	**CAMPBELL'S condensed Mushroom & Peppers *or* Cream of Mushroom Soup**
150 ml	(*¼ pt*) **milk**
450 g	(*1 lb*) **minced beef**
1 jar	(*475 g*) **tomato sauce for Spaghetti Bolognese**
75 to 100 g	(*3 to 4 oz*) **no pre-cook dried lasagne sheets**
100 g	(*4 oz*) **Cheddar cheese, grated**
	Fresh rosemary sprig for garnish

■ Preheat oven to 200 °C (*400 °F, gas mark 6*). In small bowl, combine soup and milk; set aside.

■ In large frying pan over moderate heat, gently fry mince 5 minutes or until meat is well browned, stirring to separate meat. Spoon off fat. Stir in spaghetti sauce. Heat to simmer. Reduce heat to low. Simmer gently 15 minutes, stirring occasionally.

■ Spoon ½ of meat mixture into 1.75-Lt (*3-pt*) rectangular ovenproof dish. Top with ½ of lasagne sheets and ½ of soup mixture. Repeat layers ending with soup mixture.

■ Sprinkle with Cheddar cheese. Bake 30 minutes or until golden brown and bubbling. Garnish with rosemary, if liked.

Serves 4 to 5.
Prep Time: 5 minutes
Cook Time: 55 minutes

CREAMY HOT POT

450 g	(*1 lb*) **minced beef**
1	**medium onion, finely chopped**
1 can	**CAMPBELL'S condensed Cream of Celery Soup**
200 ml	(*7 fl oz*) **milk**
15 ml	(*1 tbsp*) **Worcestershire sauce**
	Salt *and* ground black pepper
225 g	(*8 oz*) **potatoes, peeled and thinly sliced**

■ Preheat oven to 200 °C (*400 °F, gas mark 6*).

■ In large frying pan over moderate heat, gently fry mince and onion 5 minutes or until meat is well browned and onion is softened, stirring to separate meat. Spoon off fat.

■ Stir in soup, milk and Worcestershire sauce. Heat to simmer. Reduce heat to low. Simmer gently 10 minutes, stirring occasionally. Season to taste with salt and pepper.

■ Spoon into 1.15-Lt (*2-pt*) ovenproof dish. Arrange potato slices around edge of dish, overlapping slightly. Bake 30 minutes or until potatoes are tender.

TIP: If liked, place dish under a hot grill after baking to brown potatoes.

Serves 4.
Prep Time: 20 minutes
Cook Time: 45 minutes

CREAMY COTTAGE PIE

575 g	(1¼ lb) potatoes, peeled and cubed
	About 275 ml (9 fl oz) milk
50 g	(2 oz) butter or margarine
	Salt and ground black pepper
450 g	(1 lb) minced beef
1	medium onion, finely chopped
1 can	CAMPBELL'S condensed Creamy Vegetable, Mushroom & Peppers or Cream of Mushroom Soup
15 ml	(1 tbsp) Worcestershire sauce

■ In large saucepan over high heat, in boiling salted water, simmer potatoes 15 minutes or until tender. Drain; mash. Stir in *60 to 75 ml (4 to 5 tbsp)* milk and butter. Season to taste with salt and pepper.

■ Meanwhile, in large frying pan over moderate heat, gently fry mince and onion until meat is well browned and onion is softened, stirring to separate meat. Spoon off fat.

■ Stir in soup, *200 ml (7 fl oz)* milk and Worcestershire sauce. Heat to simmer. Reduce heat to low. Simmer gently 20 to 25 minutes or until meat is tender, stirring occasionally. Season to taste with salt and pepper.

■ Spoon meat mixture into warmed 1.15-Lt (2-pt) pie dish. Spread mashed potatoes over meat mixture to cover. Place under preheated medium grill until mashed potato topping is lightly browned.

TIP: To warm pie dish, place under hot running water, then dry.

Serves 4.
Prep Time: 10 minutes
Cook Time: 30 to 35 minutes

$\mathcal{P}$EPPERED STEAKS

4	**rump *or* sirloin steaks (*each* about 2 cm / 3/4 *in* thick)**
	Coarsely ground black pepper
15 ml	(*1 tbsp*) **vegetable oil**
100 g	(*4 oz*) **button mushrooms, wiped and sliced**
1 can	**CAMPBELL'S condensed Cream of Mushroom Soup**
150 ml	(*1/4 pt*) **water**
30 to 45 ml	(*2 to 3 tbsp*) **dry sherry *or* water**
	Salt *and* ground black pepper

■ Sprinkle steaks liberally on both sides with pepper.

■ In large frying pan over moderate-high heat, in hot oil, gently fry steaks 5 minutes on each side for medium, depending on thickness, or until done to taste; keep warm. Set aside.

■ Add mushrooms to same frying pan and gently fry 2 minutes. In small bowl, combine soup, water and sherry. Stir into pan. Heat to simmer. Simmer gently 3 minutes. Season to taste with salt and pepper. Serve over steaks.

Serves 4.
Prep Time: 5 minutes
Cook Time: 15 minutes

SENSATIONAL BEEF STROGANOFF

450 g	(*1 lb*) **rump steak**
30 ml	(*2 tbsp*) **vegetable oil**
1	**medium onion, finely chopped**
1 can	**CAMPBELL'S condensed Cream of Mushroom** *or* **Mushroom & Peppers Soup**
200 ml	(*7 fl oz*) **milk**
2.5 ml	(*½ tsp*) **paprika (optional)**
	Freshly cooked tagliatelle *or* **noodles**
	Chopped fresh parsley, paprika, tomato wedges *and* **fresh savory sprigs for garnish**

■ Slice steak across the grain into thin strips.

■ In large frying pan over moderate-high heat, in *15 ml* (*1 tbsp*) of hot oil, cook *half* of steak and *half* of onion until steak is no longer pink and onion is tender; set aside. Repeat with remaining oil, steak and onion. Spoon off fat.

■ Return meat mixture to frying pan. Stir in soup, milk and paprika. Heat through, stirring occasionally. Serve over tagliatelle. Sprinkle with parsley and additional paprika. Garnish with tomatoes and savory, if liked.

Turkey Stroganoff: Prepare Sensational Beef Stroganoff as directed above, *except* substitute 450 g (*1 lb*) *raw turkey breast* for the steak.

Pork Stroganoff: Prepare Sensational Beef Stroganoff as directed above, *except* substitute 450 g (*1 lb*) boneless *pork loin* for the steak.

TIP: To make slicing the meat easier, freeze steak, turkey or pork about 1 hour before cutting into thin strips.

Serves 4.
Prep Time: 10 minutes
Cook Time: 20 minutes

$\mathcal{F}$AMILY MEAT LOAF

1 can	**CAMPBELL'S condensed Cream of Mushroom *or* Cream of Tomato Soup**
675 g	**(*1½ lb*) minced beef**
75 g	**(*3 oz*) dried breadcrumbs**
½	**small onion, finely chopped**
15 ml	**(*1 tbsp*) Worcestershire sauce**
1	**(size 3) egg, beaten**
	Salt *and* ground black pepper
60 ml	**(*4 tbsp*) water**

■ In large bowl, mix thoroughly *150 ml* (*¼ pt*) of soup, mince, breadcrumbs, onion, Worcestershire sauce and egg. Season with salt and pepper. In roasting pan, *firmly* shape meat into 20- by 10-cm (*8- by 4-in*) loaf.

■ Bake at 180 °C (*350 °F, gas mark 5*) 1¼ hours or until meat loaf is thoroughly cooked and no pink remains. Spoon off fat, reserving *15 to 30 ml* (*1 to 2 tbsp*) of drippings.

■ In small saucepan over moderate heat, heat remaining soup, water and reserved drippings to simmer, stirring occasionally. Serve sauce with meat loaf.

Serves 6.
Prep Time: 15 minutes
Cook Time: 1 hour 20 minutes

$\mathcal{T}$OMATO MINCE SANDWICHES

450 g	(*1 lb*) **minced beef**
1	**small onion, thinly sliced**
1	**loaf French bread, split lengthwise***
1 can	**CAMPBELL'S condensed Consommé**
45 ml	(*3 tbsp*) **tomato ketchup**
30 ml	(*2 tbsp*) **fine cut sweet pickle**
10 ml	(*2 tsp*) **French mustard**
	Assorted toppings

■ In large frying pan over moderate heat, gently fry mince and onion until meat is well browned and onion is softened, stirring to separate meat. Spoon off fat. Meanwhile, toast French bread.

■ Stir consommé, ketchup, pickle and mustard into frying pan. Heat to simmer. Reduce heat to low. Simmer gently 20 to 25 minutes or until liquid is reduced. Fill French bread with meat mixture. Cut into four pieces. Top with assorted toppings.

TIP: Serve an assortment of toppers with this sandwich: chopped onion, lettuce, pickle and sliced tomatoes.

* For 4 individual sandwiches, use 4 hard rolls, split lengthwise.

Serves 4.
Prep Time: 10 minutes
Cook Time: 25 to 30 minutes

SWEDISH MEATBALLS

1 can	**CAMPBELL'S condensed Cream of Mushroom Soup**
150 ml	(*¹/₄ pt*) **water**
60 ml	(*4 tbsp*) **sour cream**
450 g	(*1 lb*) **lean minced beef**
40 g	(*1¹/₂ oz*) **fresh white *or* brown breadcrumbs**
1	**small onion, finely chopped**
1	(**size 3**) **egg, beaten**
1.2 ml	(*¹/₄ tsp*) **ground nutmeg**
30 ml	(*2 tbsp*) **vegetable oil**
	Freshly cooked tagliatelle
	Cherry tomatoes *and* fresh parsley for garnish

■ In small bowl, combine soup, water and sour cream; set aside.

■ In medium bowl, mix thoroughly mince, breadcrumbs, onion, egg and nutmeg. Shape mixture into 16 meatballs.

■ In large frying pan over moderate heat, in hot oil, brown meatballs, a few at a time, until thoroughly cooked and no longer pink. Spoon off fat.

■ Stir in soup mixture. Return meatballs to frying pan. Reduce heat to low. Heat through; do not boil. Serve over tagliatelle. Garnish with tomatoes and parsley, if liked.

Serves 4.
Prep Time: 20 minutes
Cook Time: 30 minutes

FOOLPROOF BEEF AND BROCCOLI

350 g	(*12 oz*) sirloin steak (about 2 cm / *3/4 in* thick)
15 ml	(*1 tbsp*) vegetable oil
1	clove garlic, peeled and crushed
150 g	(*5 oz*) broccoli florets
1	medium onion, cut into wedges
1 can	CAMPBELL'S condensed Cream of Mushroom Soup
60 ml	(*4 tbsp*) water
15 ml	(*1 tbsp*) soy sauce
	Freshly cooked tagliatelle *or* rice
	Cherry tomatoes for garnish

■ Slice steak across the grain into thin strips.

■ In large frying pan over moderate-high heat, in hot oil, gently fry steak and garlic, *half* at a time, until steak is browned. Return steak to frying pan. Add broccoli and onion. Gently fry 5 minutes, stirring regularly.

■ Stir in soup, water and soy sauce. Heat to simmer. Reduce heat to low. Cover; simmer gently 5 minutes or until vegetables are tender. Serve over tagliatelle. Garnish with cherry tomatoes, if liked.

TIP: To make slicing the meat easier, freeze steak about 1 hour before cutting into thin strips.

Serves 4.
Prep Time: 15 minutes
Cook Time: 20 minutes

FOOLPROOF BEEF AND BROCCOLI

SPICY BROCCOLI BEEF

450 g	(*1 lb*) sirloin steak (about 2 cm / *3/4 in* thick)
1 can	**CAMPBELL'S condensed Consommé**
150 ml	(*1/4 pt*) water
30 ml	(*2 tbsp*) cornflour
30 ml	(*2 tbsp*) soy sauce
1.2 ml	(*1/4 tsp*) crushed dried chillies
30 ml	(*2 tbsp*) peanut *or* vegetable oil
275 g	(*10 oz*) broccoli florets
2	spring onions, trimmed and diagonally sliced
	Freshly cooked tagliatelle *or* rice

■ Slice steak across the grain into thin strips.

■ In bowl, combine consommé, water, cornflour, soy sauce and chillies; set aside.

■ In large frying pan over high heat, in *15 ml* (*1 tbsp*) hot oil, stir-fry broccoli and spring onions 2 minutes or until tender-crisp. Transfer to bowl.

■ In same frying pan over high heat, in remaining hot oil, stir-fry steak, *half* at a time, until colour just changes. Transfer to bowl with broccoli.

■ Stir consommé mixture into frying pan. Cook over high heat until mixture simmers and thickens, stirring regularly. Add broccoli-steak mixture; heat through. Serve over tagliatelle. Serve with additional soy sauce, if liked.

Serves 4.
Prep Time: 15 minutes
Cook Time: 20 minutes

1 Combine consommé, water, cornflour, soy and chillies.

2 Stir-fry broccoli and spring onions.

3 Stir consommé mixture into frying pan and cook until thickened.

SPICY BROCCOLI BEEF

CREAMY PAN-FRIED BACON

4	**bacon chops *or* small gammon steaks**
15 ml	(*1 tbsp*) **vegetable oil**
1 can	**CAMPBELL'S condensed Ham & Cheese Soup**
200 ml	(*7 fl oz*) **milk**
5 ml	(*1 tsp*) **dried parsley**
	Salt *and* ground black pepper

■ With scissors, snip fat around chops. In large frying pan over moderate-high heat, gently fry chops 8 minutes or until lightly browned on both sides. Spoon off fat.

■ In small bowl, combine soup, milk and parsley. Stir into frying pan. Heat to simmer. Reduce heat to low. Simmer gently 5 minutes or until hot, turning chops occasionally. Season to taste with salt and pepper.

Serves 4.
Prep Time: 5 minutes
Cook Time: 15 minutes

CREAMY SOMERSET PORK

15 ml	(*1 tbsp*) **vegetable oil**
4	**pork chops (*each about 2 cm / 3/4 in thick*)**
1	**medium onion, sliced**
1 can	**CAMPBELL'S condensed Cream of Mushroom *or* Cream of Celery Soup**
200 ml	(*7 fl oz*) **water *or* dry cider**
1	**eating apple, peeled, quartered, cored and sliced**
5 ml	(*1 tsp*) **dried sage**
	Salt *and* ground black pepper

■ In large frying pan over moderate-high heat, in hot oil, gently fry chops and onion 10 minutes or until chops are browned on both sides and onion is softened.

■ In medium bowl, combine soup, water, apple and sage. Stir into frying pan. Heat to simmer. Reduce heat to low. Simmer gently 15 minutes or until chops are tender. Season to taste with salt and pepper.

Serves 4.
Prep Time: 10 minutes
Cook Time: 30 minutes

Garden Pork Sauté

25 g	(*1 oz*) **butter** *or* **margarine**
4	**boneless pork chops** (*each* **about 2 cm /** *3/4 in* **thick**)
75 g	(*3 oz*) **broccoli florets**
75 g	(*3 oz*) **button mushrooms, wiped and sliced**
50 g	(*2 oz*) **diagonally sliced, peeled carrot**
1 can	**CAMPBELL'S condensed Cream of Chicken Soup**
75 ml	(*3 fl oz*) **milk**
3	**rindless rashers bacon, cooked and crumbled**
	Pinch ground black pepper
	Freshly cooked tagliatelle (optional)

■ In large frying pan over moderate-high heat, in *15 g* (*1/2 oz*) of hot butter, gently fry pork chops 10 minutes or until browned on both sides. Remove chops; keep warm.

■ In same frying pan, in remaining butter, gently fry broccoli, mushrooms and carrot 5 minutes, stirring regularly. Stir in soup, milk, bacon and pepper. Heat to simmer.

■ Return chops to frying pan. Reduce heat to low. Simmer gently 5 minutes or until chops are tender. Serve with tagliatelle, if liked.

Serves 4.
Prep Time: 20 minutes
Cook Time: 25 minutes

1 Gently fry chops 10 minutes in frying pan.

2 Remove chops and keep warm.

GARDEN PORK SAUTÉ

3   Add vegetables to frying pan.

4   Stir in soup, milk and bacon.

TORTELLINI WITH MUSHROOMS AND HAM

250 g	(*9 oz*) **dried cheese-filled tortellini***
15 ml	(*1 tbsp*) **olive oil**
75 g	(*3 oz*) **ham, cut into strips**
½	**small onion, chopped**
1	**clove garlic, peeled and crushed**
2.5 ml	(*½ tsp*) **dried basil**
1 can	**CAMPBELL'S condensed Cream of Mushroom Soup**
300 ml	(*½ pt*) **milk**
150 g	(*5 oz*) **frozen peas**
30 ml	(*2 tbsp*) **chopped fresh parsley**
	Pinch ground black pepper
	Grated Parmesan cheese
	Red pepper strips for garnish

■ Cook tortellini according to packet directions. Drain. Meanwhile, in medium saucepan over moderate heat, in hot oil, gently fry ham, onion, garlic and basil 2 minutes, stirring regularly.

■ Stir in soup, milk, peas, parsley and pepper. Heat to simmer. Reduce heat to low. Cover; simmer gently 5 minutes or until peas are tender. Stir in tortellini.

■ Serve with Parmesan cheese. Garnish with red pepper strips, if liked.

* If not available at your food store, substitute 100 g (4 oz) dried pasta twists for the tortellini.

Serves 4.
Prep Time: 15 minutes
Cook Time: 10 to 15 minutes

TORTELLINI WITH MUSHROOMS AND HAM

SAUCY SAUSAGES AND ONION

15 ml	(*1 tbsp*) vegetable oil
450 g	(*1 lb*) pork sausages
1	medium onion, sliced
1 can	CAMPBELL's condensed Cream of Mushroom *or* Cream of Celery Soup
200 ml	(*7 fl oz*) water
5 ml	(*1 tsp*) prepared English *or* French mustard (optional)
	Salt *and* ground black pepper

■ In large frying pan over moderate heat, in hot oil, gently fry sausages and onion 12 to 15 minutes or until sausages are lightly browned and onion is softened, turning regularly.

■ In small bowl, combine soup, water and mustard. Stir into frying pan. Heat to simmer. Reduce heat to low. Simmer gently 5 minutes or until hot, stirring occasionally. Season to taste with salt and pepper.

Serves 4.
Prep Time: 5 minutes
Cook Time: 25 to 30 minutes

GLORIFIED PORK CHOPS

15 ml	(*1 tbsp*) vegetable oil
6	pork chops (*each about 2 cm / 3/4 in thick*)
1 can	CAMPBELL'S condensed Cream of Celery *or* Cream of Mushroom Soup
150 ml	(*1/4 pt*) water
	Sliced tomato *and* fresh parsley sprigs for garnish

■ In large frying pan over moderate-high heat, in hot oil, gently fry chops, *half* at a time, 10 minutes or until browned on both sides. Remove; set aside. Repeat with remaining chops. Spoon off fat.

■ Stir soup and water into frying pan. Heat to simmer. Return chops to frying pan. Reduce heat to low. Cover; simmer gently 10 to 15 minutes or until chops are tender, stirring occasionally. Garnish with tomato and parsley, if liked.

Onion Glorified Pork Chops: Prepare Glorified Pork Chops as directed above, *except* gently fry 1 medium *onion*, sliced, with chops.

Savoury Glorified Pork Chops: Prepare Glorified Pork Chops as directed above, *except* add 5 ml (*1 tsp*) *Worcestershire sauce* with the soup.

Mushroom Glorified Pork Chops: Prepare Glorified Pork Chops as directed above, *except* use only the *Cream of Mushroom Soup*. Add 100 g (*4 oz*) sliced, wiped *button mushrooms* with the soup.

Serves 6.
Prep Time: 5 minutes
Cook Time: 35 to 40 minutes

PLUM GLAZED GAMMON

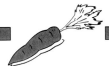

*P*LUM GLAZED GAMMON

1	**boneless smoked gammon joint [about 2.2 kg (*5 lb*)]**
45 ml	(*3 tbsp*) **cornflour**
1 can	**CAMPBELL'S condensed Consommé**
1 can (570 g)	(*20 oz*) **plums, drained, stoned and halved**
75 g	(*6 oz*) **orange marmalade**
30 ml	(*2 tbsp*) **prepared English mustard**
	Orange slices for garnish

■ On rack in roasting pan, place gammon fat-side up. With sharp knife, score fat into 1½-cm (*¾-in*) squares. (Insert meat thermometer into thickest part of meat.) Bake at 160 °C (*325 °F, gas mark 3*) 45 minutes.

■ Meanwhile, reserve 6 to 8 plum halves; purée remaining plums. In medium saucepan, stir together cornflour and consommé until smooth. Stir in plum purée, marmalade and mustard. Over high heat, heat to simmer, stirring regularly. Reduce heat to moderate; simmer gently 5 minutes, stirring occasionally until sauce is slightly thickened. Brush *175 ml* (*6 fl oz*) sauce over gammon; set remaining sauce aside.

■ Bake gammon 1 hour more or until thermometer reads 60 °C (*140 °F*), basting occasionally with sauce. Let stand 10 minutes before carving. Heat remaining sauce. Serve with gammon. Garnish with additional plum halves and orange slices, if liked.

Serves 10 to 14.
Prep Time: 20 minutes
Cook Time: 1 hour 45 minutes

HERBED PORK CHOPS

30 ml	(*2 tbsp*) plain flour
1.2 ml	(*1/4 tsp*) dried sage
1.2 ml	(*1/4 tsp*) dried thyme
4	boneless pork chops (*each* about 2 cm / *3/4 in* thick)
25 g	(*1 oz*) butter *or* margarine
1 can	CAMPBELL'S condensed Cream of Chicken Soup
150 ml	(*1/4 pt*) water
	Freshly cooked long-grain and wild rice mix *or* freshly cooked rice
	Fresh thyme sprigs, orange slices *and* radicchio leaves for garnish

■ On plate, combine flour, sage and thyme. Coat chops lightly with flour mixture.

■ In large frying pan over moderate-high heat, in hot butter, gently fry chops 10 minutes or until browned on both sides. Push chops to one side of frying pan.

■ Stir in soup and water, stirring to loosen browned bits. Heat to simmer. Reduce heat to low. Simmer gently 15 minutes or until chops are tender. Serve chops with rice; spoon sauce over. Garnish with thyme, orange slices and radicchio, if liked.

Serves 4.
Prep Time: 10 minutes
Cook Time: 25 minutes

1 Combine flour, sage and thyme.

2 Coat chops lightly with flour mixture.

3 Gently fry chops in hot butter.

4 Stir in soup and water.

HERBED PORK CHOPS

TOMATO-BASIL PORK CHOPS

15 ml	(*1 tbsp*) olive oil
4	boneless pork chops (*each* about 2 cm / 3/4 *in* thick)
1 can	CAMPBELL'S condensed Cream of Tomato Soup
150 ml	(*1/4 pt*) water
1	medium onion, finely chopped
2.5 ml	(*1/2 tsp*) dried basil
	Ground black pepper
1	orange, sliced
1	medium green pepper, de-seeded and cut into strips
	Freshly cooked wild *or* white rice

■ In large frying pan over moderate-high heat, in hot oil, gently fry chops about 10 minutes or until browned on both sides. Remove chops; keep warm. Spoon off fat.

■ Stir soup, water, onion and basil into frying pan. Season to taste with black pepper. Add orange and green pepper. Heat to simmer. Return chops to frying pan. Reduce heat to low. Simmer gently 10 to 15 minutes or until chops are tender, stirring occasionally. Serve over rice.

Serves 4.
Prep Time: 15 minutes
Cook Time: 25 to 30 minutes

BAVARIAN HAM WITH NOODLES

175 g	(*6 oz*) dried tagliatelle
15 ml	(*1 tbsp*) vegetable oil
350 g	(*12 oz*) diced ham
1	large onion, sliced
1 can	CAMPBELL'S condensed Cream of Mushroom Soup
300 ml	(*½ pt*) milk
175 g	(*6 oz*) frozen cut green beans
	Ground black pepper
	French mustard

■ Cook tagliatelle according to packet directions. Drain. Meanwhile, in large frying pan over moderate heat, in hot oil, gently fry ham and onion until ham is browned and onion is softened, stirring regularly. Spoon off fat.

■ Stir in soup. Gradually stir in milk. Add beans. Season to taste with pepper. Heat to simmer. Reduce heat to low. Simmer gently 5 minutes or until beans are tender, stirring occasionally.

■ Stir cooked tagliatelle into frying pan. Heat 2 minutes, stirring regularly. Serve with mustard, if liked.

Serves 4.
Prep Time: 15 minutes
Cook Time: 15 minutes

LAMB PASANDA

1 can	**CAMPBELL'S condensed Mushroom & Peppers Soup**
200 ml	(*7 fl oz*) **milk**
45 ml	(*3 tbsp*) **mild curry paste**
15 ml	(*1 tbsp*) **mango chutney (optional)**
450 g	(*1 lb*) **boneless leg of lamb, cut into 2.5-cm (*1-in*) cubes**
1	**small onion, finely chopped**
	Freshly cooked rice

■ In 2-Lt (*3½-pt*) casserole dish, combine soup, milk, curry paste and chutney. Stir in lamb and onion; cover.

■ Bake at 200 °C (*400 °F, gas mark 6*) for 1¼ hours or until lamb is tender, stirring occasionally. Serve over rice.

Serves 4.
Prep Time: 10 minutes
Cook Time: 1¼ hours

$\mathcal{M}$INTED LAMB CHOPS

8	**lamb loin chops**
10 ml	(*2 tsp*) **dried mint**
15 ml	(*1 tbsp*) **vegetable oil**
1	**medium onion, finely chopped**
1 can	**CAMPBELL'S condensed Cream of Celery Soup**
200 ml	(*7 fl oz*) **milk**
	Salt *and* ground black pepper

■ Sprinkle chops on both sides with mint. Place chops on grill pan. Place under preheated medium grill 7 to 8 minutes on each side or until done.

■ Meanwhile, in medium saucepan over moderate heat, in hot oil, gently fry onion until softened. Stir in soup and milk. Simmer gently 5 minutes, stirring regularly. Season to taste with salt and pepper. Serve over chops.

Serves 4.
Prep Time: 5 minutes
Cook Time: 15 minutes

$\mathcal{R}$AGOUT OF VEAL AND MUSHROOMS

675 g	(1¹/₂ lb) veal, cut into 4-cm (1¹/₂-in) pieces
30 ml	(2 tbsp) olive oil
25 g	(1 oz) butter or margarine
1	large onion, quartered lengthwise and thinly sliced
225 g	(8 oz) button mushrooms, wiped and sliced (optional)
2.5 ml	(¹/₂ tsp) dried thyme
150 ml	(¹/₄ pt) dry sherry
1 can	CAMPBELL'S condensed Cream of Mushroom Soup
150 ml	(¹/₄ pt) water
15 ml	(1 tbsp) paprika
	Ground black pepper
	Freshly cooked rice

■ Trim excess fat from veal. With flat side of meat mallet or rolling pin, pound meat to flatten slightly.

■ In large saucepan over moderate heat, in 15 ml (1 tbsp) hot oil and 15 g (¹/₂ oz) butter, gently fry veal, a few pieces at a time, until browned on all sides. Set aside.

■ To hot fat add remaining oil and butter. Over moderate heat, gently fry onion, mushrooms and thyme until softened, stirring occasionally. Add sherry.

■ Stir in soup, water and paprika. Return veal and any accumulated juices to saucepan. Reduce heat to low. Cover; simmer gently 1 hour, stirring occasionally.

■ Uncover, simmer gently about 20 minutes more or until veal is tender and sauce is desired consistency, stirring regularly. Season to taste with pepper. Serve with rice.

Serves 4 to 6.
Prep Time: 35 minutes
Cook Time: 1 hour 30 minutes

RAGOUT OF VEAL AND MUSHROOMS

*T*UNA AND PEPPER SPAGHETTI

350 g	(*12 oz*) dried spaghetti
1 can	CAMPBELL'S condensed Mushroom & Peppers Soup
150 ml	(*¼ pt*) milk
1 can (198 g)	(*7 oz*) tuna, drained and flaked
100 g	(*4 oz*) Cheddar cheese, grated
	Salt *and* ground black pepper

■ Cook spaghetti according to packet directions. Drain.

■ In large saucepan, combine soup and milk. Add cooked spaghetti, tuna and Cheddar cheese. Over low heat, simmer gently 5 minutes or until heated through, tossing and stirring regularly. Season to taste with salt and pepper.

Serves 4.
Prep Time: 20 minutes
Cook Time: 25 to 30 minutes

PRAWN VOL AU VENTS

6	**frozen king-size vol au vent cases**
25 g	(*1 oz*) **butter *or* margarine**
150 g	(*5 oz*) **button mushrooms, wiped and sliced**
1 can	**CAMPBELL'S condensed Cream of Celery Soup**
50 g	(*2 oz*) **frozen peas**
45 ml	(*3 tbsp*) **dry sherry *or* water**
350 g	(*12 oz*) **large, peeled prawns (thawed if frozen)**
	Celery leaves for garnish

■ Preheat oven and bake vol au vent cases according to packet directions; keep warm.

■ Meanwhile, in large frying pan over moderate heat, in hot butter, gently fry mushrooms until softened and liquid is evaporated, stirring occasionally.

■ Stir in soup, peas and sherry. Heat to simmer. Simmer gently 4 minutes. Stir in prawns. Heat through. Spoon prawn mixture over vol au vent cases. Garnish with *celery leaves*, if liked.

Serves 6.
Prep Time: 25 minutes
Cook Time: 15 minutes

CREAMY DILL SALMON STEAKS

15 g	(½ oz) butter or margarine
4	spring onions, trimmed and chopped
1 can	CAMPBELL'S condensed Cream of Celery or Cream of Asparagus Soup
150 ml	(¼ pt) single cream
30 ml	(2 tbsp) dry white wine
30 ml	(2 tbsp) chopped fresh dill or 5 ml (1 tsp) dried dill weed
4	salmon steaks, (each about 2.5 cm / 1 in thick)
	Fresh dill for garnish
	Freshly cooked wild or white rice

■ In large frying pan over moderate heat, in hot butter, gently fry spring onions until softened, stirring regularly. Stir in soup, cream, wine and dill.

■ Arrange fish steaks in soup mixture. Heat to simmer. Reduce heat to low. Cover; simmer gently 15 minutes or until fish flakes easily when tested with fork. Serve fish with sauce. Garnish with fresh dill, if liked. Serve with rice.

To microwave: In 30- by 20-cm (*12- by 8-in*) microwave-proof dish, combine butter and onions. Cover; microwave on HIGH 2 minutes or until onions are softened, stirring once during cooking. Stir in soup, cream, wine and dill. Arrange fish steaks in dish with thicker portions of fish toward outside of dish. Cover; microwave on HIGH 10 to 11 minutes or until fish flakes easily when tested with fork, rotating dish twice during cooking. Let stand, covered, 5 minutes before serving.

Serves 4.
Prep Time: 10 minutes
Cook Time: 25 minutes

CREAMY DILL SALMON STEAKS

PAN-FRIED FISH

450 g	(*1 lb*) thick fresh cod *or* haddock fillet, skinned and cut into 4-cm (*1½-in*) cubes
25 g	(*1 oz*) plain flour seasoned with salt *and* ground black pepper
30 ml	(*2 tbsp*) vegetable oil
1 can	CAMPBELL'S condensed Mushroom & Peppers Soup
150 ml	(*¼ pt*) milk
75 g	(*3 oz*) frozen peas
15 ml	(*1 tbsp*) lemon juice
	Salt *and* ground black pepper

■ On plate, toss fish with seasoned flour. In large frying pan over moderate heat, in hot oil, gently fry fish until lightly browned, turning carefully.

■ In small bowl, combine soup and milk. Stir soup mixture, peas and lemon juice into frying pan. Simmer gently 5 minutes or until fish flakes easily when tested with fork and peas are tender, stirring occasionally. Season to taste with salt and pepper.

Serves 4.
Prep Time: 10 minutes
Cook Time: 10 minutes

*F*ISH WITH LEMON SAUCE

1 can	**CAMPBELL'S condensed Cream of Celery Soup**
150 ml	**(^{1}/$_4$ *pt*) milk**
	Finely grated rind *and* juice of 1/2 lemon
	Salt *and* ground black pepper
450 g	**(*1 lb*) fresh cod *or* haddock fillet, skinned and cut into 4 portions**

■ Preheat oven to 190 °C (*375 °F, gas mark 5*).

■ In small bowl, combine soup, milk, lemon rind and lemon juice. Season to taste with salt and pepper. Arrange fish in shallow 1.15-Lt (*2-pt*) ovenproof dish. Pour sauce over fish; cover. Bake 25 minutes or until fish flakes easily when tested with fork.

Serves 4.
Prep Time: 5 minutes
Cook Time: 25 minutes

CREAMY FISH WITH CRUMB TOPPING

1 can	**CAMPBELL'S condensed Cream of Celery Soup**
150 ml	(*¼ pt*) **milk**
75 g	(*3 oz*) **frozen peas**
450 g	(*1 lb*) **fresh cod** *or* **haddock fillet, skinned and cut into 2.5-cm** (*1-in*) **cubes***
15 ml	(*1 tbsp*) **chopped fresh parsley (optional)**
	Salt *and* **ground black pepper**
75 g	(*3 oz*) **Cheddar cheese, grated**
50 g	(*2 oz*) **fresh white** *or* **brown breadcrumbs**

■ In large saucepan, combine soup, milk and peas. Over moderate heat, gently heat through, stirring regularly. Add fish and parsley. Simmer gently 8 to 10 minutes or until fish flakes easily when tested with fork, stirring occasionally. Season to taste with salt and pepper.

■ Spoon into warmed 1.15-Lt (*2-pt*) ovenproof dish. In small bowl, mix Cheddar cheese with breadcrumbs. Sprinkle over fish mixture. Place under hot grill 5 minutes or until topping is golden brown.

TIP: To warm dish, place under hot running water, then dry.

* *You can substitute a frozen, thawed cod or haddock fillet for the fresh fillet.*

Serves 4.
Prep Time: 10 minutes
Cook Time: 15 minutes

$\mathcal{T}$UNA AND SWEETCORN BAKE

275 g	(***10 oz***) **dried pasta shells**
1 can	**CAMPBELL'S condensed Cream of Celery Soup**
200 ml	(***7 fl oz***) **milk**
2 cans (198 g each)	(***7 oz*** **each) tuna, drained and flaked**
1 can (330 g)	(***11½ oz***) **sweetcorn, drained**
75 g	(***3 oz***) **Cheddar cheese, grated**

■ Preheat oven to 200 °C (*400 °F, gas mark 6*). Cook pasta shells according to packet directions. Drain.

■ In 1.75-Lt (*3-pt*) shallow ovenproof dish, combine soup and milk. Stir in tuna, sweetcorn and cooked pasta shells. Sprinkle with Cheddar cheese.

■ Bake 20 to 25 minutes or until hot and bubbling.

Serves 4.
Prep Time: 15 minutes
Cook Time: 20 to 25 minutes

*F*ISH WITH EMMENTAL CHEESE SAUCE

6	**small plaice fillets**
1 can	**CAMPBELL'S condensed Cream of Mushroom Soup**
30 ml	(*2 tbsp*) **dry white wine**
50 g	(*2 oz*) **Emmental cheese, grated**
15 ml	(*1 tbsp*) **chopped fresh parsley**

■ Preheat oven to 200 °C (*400 °F, gas mark 6*).

■ In 33- by 23-cm (*13- by 9-in*) shallow ovenproof dish, arrange fish fillets in a single layer. Bake 10 minutes.

■ Meanwhile, in small bowl, combine soup and wine. Stir any accumulated juices from fish into soup mixture; pour over fillets. Sprinkle with Emmental cheese and parsley. Bake 5 to 10 minutes more or until fish flakes easily when tested with fork and sauce is hot.

Serves 6.
Prep Time: 10 minutes
Cook Time: 15 to 20 minutes

CREAMY MUSHROOM SAUCE FOR FISH

1 can	**CAMPBELL'S condensed Cream of Mushroom Soup**
150 ml	**(¼ pt) milk *or* water**

■ In small saucepan, combine soup and milk. Over moderate heat, heat through, stirring regularly. Serve over cooked fish.

To microwave: In small microwave-proof dish, combine soup and milk. Microwave on HIGH 2½ minutes or until hot, stirring halfway through heating.

Makes about 450 ml (¾ pt).
Prep Time: 5 minutes
Cook Time: 5 minutes

TOMATO AND ONION SAUCE FOR FISH

1 can	**CAMPBELL'S condensed Tomato & Onion Soup**
150 ml	**(¼ pt) water *or* dry white wine**

■ In small saucepan, combine soup and water. Over moderate heat, heat through, stirring regularly. Serve over cooked fish or seafood.

To microwave: In small microwave-proof dish, combine soup and water. Microwave on HIGH 2½ minutes or until hot, stirring halfway through heating.

Makes about 450 ml (¾ pt).
Prep Time: 5 minutes
Cook Time: 5 minutes

CHEESY TUNA AND TWISTS

225 g	(8 oz) dried pasta twists
25 g	(1 oz) butter or margarine
275 g	(10 oz) frozen mixed vegetables, thawed
1	clove garlic, peeled and crushed
1 can	CAMPBELL'S condensed Cream of Mushroom or Mushroom & Peppers Soup
150 ml	(¼ pt) milk
175 g	(6 oz) mozzarella cheese, grated
	Generous pinch ground nutmeg
	Salt and ground black pepper
1 can (198 g)	(7 oz) tuna, drained

■ Cook pasta twists according to packet directions. Drain.

■ In large frying pan over moderate heat, in hot butter, gently fry mixed vegetables and garlic 2 minutes, stirring regularly.

■ Add soup to frying pan; stir until smooth. Gradually stir in milk, mozzarella cheese and nutmeg. Season to taste with salt and pepper. Heat until cheese melts, stirring occasionally.

■ Stir in cooked pasta twists and tuna. Heat through.

TIP: For a heartier cheese flavour, use mature Cheddar instead of mozzarella.

Serves 4.
Prep Time: 20 minutes
Cook Time: 15 minutes

1 Gently fry vegetables and garlic in hot butter.

2 Add soup to frying pan and mix well.

CHEESY TUNA AND TWISTS

3 Gradually stir in milk. Add mozzarella cheese and nutmeg.

4 Stir in tuna and cooked pasta twists.

TUNA TAGLIATELLE CASSEROLE

*T*UNA TAGLIATELLE CASSEROLE

175 g	**(*6 oz*) dried tagliatelle**
25 g	**(*1 oz*) butter *or* margarine**
1	**small onion, chopped**
1 can	**CAMPBELL'S condensed Cream of Mushroom Soup**
150 ml	**(*¼ pt*) milk**
2 cans (198 g each)	**(*7 oz* each) tuna, drained and flaked**
150 g	**(*5 oz*) frozen peas, cooked**
50 g	**(*2 oz*) Cheddar cheese, grated**

■ Preheat oven to 200 °C (*400 °F, gas mark 6*).

■ Cook tagliatelle according to packet directions. Drain.

■ In medium saucepan over moderate heat, in hot butter, gently fry onion until softened. Stir in soup, milk, tuna and peas. Add cooked tagliatelle; toss to coat well. Spoon into 1.4-Lt (*2½-pt*) ovenproof dish.

■ Bake 25 minutes or until hot; stir. Sprinkle with Cheddar cheese. Bake 5 minutes more or until cheese melts.

Serves 4.
Prep Time: 15 minutes
Cook Time: 35 minutes

SAUCY CHEESE TORTELLINI

250 g	**(9 oz) dried cheese-filled tortellini***
1 can	**CAMPBELL'S condensed Cream of Mushroom Soup**
300 ml	**(1/2 pt) milk**
100 g	**(4 oz) frozen peas**
50 g	**(2 oz) grated, peeled carrot**
	Freshly ground black pepper
45 ml	**(3 tbsp) grated Parmesan cheese**
45 ml	**(3 tbsp) chopped fresh parsley**
	Chopped toasted walnuts for garnish

■ Cook tortellini according to packet directions. Drain.

■ Meanwhile, in large saucepan, combine soup, milk, peas and carrot. Season to taste with pepper. Over moderate heat, heat to simmer. Reduce heat to low. Cover; simmer gently 4 minutes or until peas are tender, stirring occasionally.

■ Stir in Parmesan cheese and parsley. Heat until Parmesan cheese melts. Stir in cooked tortellini. Garnish with walnuts, if liked.

* If not available at your food store, substitute 100 g (4 oz) dried pasta twists for the tortellini.

Serves 4 as a main dish.
Prep Time: 10 minutes
Cook Time: 15 minutes

*E*GGS DIJON WITH ASPARAGUS

1 pkt (250 g)	**(8.8 oz) frozen asparagus** *or* **broccoli spears, thawed and cut-up**
1 can	**CAMPBELL'S condensed Cream of Chicken Soup**
150 ml	**(1/4 pt) milk**
2.5 ml	**(1/2 tsp) Dijon mustard**
	Generous pinch ground black pepper
4	**(size 3) hard-boiled eggs, shelled and coarsely chopped**
100 g	**(4 oz) Emmental cheese, grated**
4	**English muffins, halved and toasted** *or* **8 slices bread, toasted**

■ In covered medium saucepan over moderate heat, in 2.5 cm (*1 in*) boiling water, gently simmer asparagus 3 minutes. Drain.

■ Meanwhile, in small saucepan, combine soup, milk, mustard and pepper. Add eggs and Emmental cheese. Over moderate heat, heat through, stirring occasionally.

■ On *each* of 4 plates, place 2 muffin halves; top with asparagus and spoon egg mixture over.

Serves 4 as a starter.
Prep Time: 20 minutes
Cook Time: 10 minutes

CHEESY MUSHROOM FRITTATA

1 can	**CAMPBELL'S condensed Cream of Mushroom Soup**
6	**(size 3) eggs, lightly beaten**
175 g	**(6 oz) mozzarella cheese, grated**
1.2 ml	**(¼ tsp) dried basil**
	Salt and ground black pepper
25 g	**(1 oz) butter or margarine**
75 g	**(3 oz) button mushrooms, wiped and sliced**
1	**medium onion, chopped**
	Chopped fresh parsley, tomato wedges and fresh basil leaves for garnish

■ In medium bowl with wire whisk, beat soup. Gradually blend in eggs, 75 g (3 oz) mozzarella cheese and basil. Season with salt and pepper. Set aside.

■ In large flame-proof frying pan over moderate heat, in hot butter, gently fry mushrooms and onion until mushrooms are softened and liquid is evaporated, stirring occasionally.

■ Pour soup mixture into frying pan. Reduce heat to low. Cook 6 minutes or until eggs are set 2.5 cm (1 in) from edge. *Do not stir.* Remove from heat.

■ Place under medium grill 5 minutes or until frittata is puffy and lightly browned. Top with remaining mozzarella cheese. Cover; let stand 2 minutes or until cheese melts. Garnish with parsley, tomato wedges and basil, if liked.

Serves 4 to 5 as a main dish.
Prep Time: 15 minutes
Cook Time: 15 minutes

CHEESY MUSHROOM FRITTATA

QUICK QUICHE

19-cm	(7½-in) ready-made pastry flan case
4	(size 3) eggs
1 can	CAMPBELL'S condensed Ham & Cheese Soup
25 g	(1 oz) Cheddar cheese, grated

■ Preheat oven to 190 °C (375 °F, gas mark 5). Place flan case on baking tray.

■ In large bowl, beat eggs. Gradually stir in soup. Pour into flan case. Sprinkle with Cheddar cheese. Bake 35 minutes or until golden brown and set. Serve warm or cold.

Serves 4.
Prep Time: 5 minutes
Cook Time: 35 minutes

SHORTCUT EGGS BENEDICT

1 can	**CAMPBELL'S condensed Cream of Chicken *or* Ham & Cheese Soup**
60 ml	**(*4 tbsp*) milk**
15 ml	**(*1 tbsp*) lemon juice**
12	**rindless rashers streaky bacon, cooked and drained**
3	**English muffins, halved and toasted *or* 6 slices bread, toasted**
6	**poached eggs**
15 ml	**(*1 tbsp*) chopped fresh parsley**

■ In medium saucepan, combine soup, milk and lemon juice. Over low heat, gently heat through, stirring occasionally.

■ Meanwhile, place 2 rashers of bacon on each English muffin half; top each with 1 egg.

■ Pour *45 ml* (*3 tbsp*) of sauce over each egg and sprinkle with parsley. Serve immediately.

To microwave: In 1.15-Lt (*2-pt*) microwave-proof dish, combine soup, milk and lemon juice. Cover; microwave on HIGH 4 minutes or until hot, stirring halfway through cooking. Continue as directed above.

Serves 6 as a starter.
Prep Time: 10 minutes
Cook Time: 5 minutes

GINGERED VEGETABLES

15 ml	(*1 tbsp*) **vegetable oil**
100 g	(*4 oz*) **diagonally sliced, peeled carrots**
100 g	(*4 oz*) **diagonally sliced, trimmed celery**
1	**small red pepper, de-seeded and cut into strips**
1	**medium onion, roughly chopped**
75 ml	(*3 oz*) **mangetout**
50 g	(*2 oz*) **broccoli florets**
1	**clove garlic, peeled and crushed**
2.5 ml	(*½ tsp*) **ground ginger**
30 ml	(*2 tbsp*) **cornflour**
1 can	**CAMPBELL'S condensed Consommé**

■ In large frying pan or wok over high heat, in hot oil, stir-fry carrots, celery, red pepper and onion 3 minutes.

■ Add mangetout, broccoli, garlic and ginger. Sprinkle cornflour over vegetables. Stir in consommé. Heat to simmer, stirring regularly. Simmer gently until mixture boils and thickens, stirring regularly. Reduce heat to low. Cover; simmer until vegetables are tender-crisp.

■ Serve with *soy sauce*, if liked.

To microwave: Omit oil. In 2-Lt (*3½-pt*) microwave-proof dish, combine vegetables and garlic. Cover; microwave on HIGH 7 minutes or until vegetables are tender-crisp, stirring once during cooking. Sprinkle cornflour over vegetables. Stir in ginger and consommé until blended. Cover; microwave on HIGH 4 minutes or until thickened, stirring halfway through cooking. Serve as directed above.

Serves 4.
Cook Time: 10 minutes
Prep Time: 15 minutes

1 Stir-fry carrots, celery, red pepper and onion.

GINGERED VEGETABLES

2 Add mangetout, broccoli, garlic and ginger.

3 Sprinkle cornflour over vegetables.

4 Stir in consommé. Heat to simmer, stirring regularly.

QUICK RICE AND BEANS

3	**rindless rashers bacon, diced**
1	**clove garlic, peeled and crushed**
1.2 ml	**(¼ tsp) ground coriander**
1.2 ml	**(¼ tsp) ground cumin**
200 g	**(7 oz) uncooked long-grain rice**
1 can (440 g)	**(15½ oz) chick peas or red kidney beans, drained**
1 can	**CAMPBELL'S condensed Consommé**
150 ml	**(¼ pt) water**
1	**bay leaf**
	Generous pinch ground black pepper

■ In medium saucepan over moderate-high heat, gently fry bacon until crisp. Spoon off fat. Add garlic, coriander and cumin. Cook 1 minute, stirring regularly.

■ Stir in rice, chick peas, consommé, water, bay leaf and pepper. Heat to simmer. Reduce heat to low. Cover; simmer gently 20 minutes or until rice is tender and liquid is absorbed. Remove bay leaf; discard. Garnish with *fresh bay leaves*, if liked.

Serves 6 to 8.
Prep Time: 10 minutes
Cook Time: 30 minutes

TOMATO COURGETTE MEDLEY

1 can	**CAMPBELL'S condensed Cream of Tomato Soup**
45 ml	(*3 tbsp*) **grated Parmesan cheese**
15 ml	(*1 tbsp*) **lemon juice**
2.5 ml	(*½ tsp*) **garlic granules**
2.5 ml	(*½ tsp*) **dried basil**
675 g	(*1½ lb*) **courgettes, trimmed and sliced**
1	**medium onion, thinly sliced**
1	**green pepper, de-seeded and cut into strips**

■ In large saucepan, combine soup, Parmesan cheese, lemon juice, garlic granules and basil. Add courgettes, onion and green pepper. Toss to coat well.

■ Over moderate heat, heat to simmer. Reduce heat to low. Cover; simmer gently 10 minutes or until vegetables are tender, stirring occasionally. Top with additional *Parmesan cheese*, if liked.

To microwave: In 30- by 20-cm (*12- by 8-in*) microwave-proof dish, combine ingredients as directed above. Cover with baking parchment. Microwave on HIGH 15 minutes, stirring halfway through cooking. Continue as directed above.

Serves 6 to 8.
Prep Time: 15 minutes
Cook Time: 15 minutes

CURRY-SAUCED CAULIFLOWER

CURRY-SAUCED CAULIFLOWER

450 g	(*1 lb*) cauliflower florets
1 can	CAMPBELL'S condensed Cream of Celery Soup
150 ml	(*¼ pt*) milk
50 g	(*2 oz*) Cheddar cheese, grated
10 ml	(*2 tsp*) mild curry paste
	Generous pinch ground black pepper
150 g	(*5 oz*) frozen peas, thawed
1	small red pepper, de-seeded and diced
	Toasted flaked almonds for garnish

■ In large frying pan over moderate heat, in 1 cm (*½ in*) boiling water, simmer cauliflower 5 minutes or until tender-crisp. Drain.

■ In same frying pan, combine soup, milk, Cheddar cheese, curry paste and pepper. Add cauliflower, peas and red pepper. Over moderate heat, simmer gently 5 minutes or until vegetables are tender, stirring regularly. Garnish with almonds.

To microwave: In 2-Lt (*3½-pt*) medium microwave-proof dish, place cauliflower in 1 cm (*½ in*) water. Cover; microwave on HIGH 10 minutes or until tender-crisp. Drain. In same dish, stir soup, milk, Cheddar cheese, curry paste and pepper until smooth. Add cooked cauliflower, peas and red pepper. Cover; microwave on HIGH 3 minutes or until vegetables are tender and cheese melts, stirring once during cooking. Garnish as directed above.

TIP: A great make-ahead recipe—just reheat in your microwave oven.

Serves 6 to 8.
Prep Time: 10 minutes
Cook Time: 15 minutes

CREAMY MUSHROOM PILAF

25 g	(*1 oz*) **butter *or* margarine**
1	**small onion, chopped**
200 g	(*7 oz*) *uncooked* **long-grain rice**
75 g	(*3 oz*) **button mushrooms, wiped and sliced**
1 can	**CAMPBELL'S condensed Cream of Chicken Soup**
300 ml	(*½ pt*) **water**
60 ml	(*4 tbsp*) **dry white wine *or* dry sherry**
	Salt *and* ground black pepper
30 ml	(*2 tbsp*) **sour cream**
50 g	(*2 oz*) **grated Parmesan cheese**
15 ml	(*1 tbsp*) **chopped fresh parsley for garnish**

■ In medium saucepan over moderate heat, in hot butter, gently fry onion, rice and mushrooms 5 minutes or until rice is lightly browned, stirring regularly.

■ Stir in soup, water and wine. Season to taste with salt and pepper. Heat to simmer. Reduce heat to low. Cover; simmer gently 20 minutes, stirring occasionally. Remove from heat.

■ Stir in sour cream and *half* of Parmesan cheese. Cover; let stand 5 minutes or until all liquid is absorbed. Garnish with remaining Parmesan cheese and parsley.

To microwave: Place butter in 2-Lt (*3½-pt*) microwave-proof dish, microwave on HIGH 1 minute until melted. Stir in onion, mushrooms and rice. Microwave on HIGH 5 minutes until rice is lightly browned, stirring once during cooking. Stir in soup, water and wine. Season to taste with salt and pepper. Cover. Microwave on HIGH 6 to 8 minutes until mixture simmers. Microwave at 50% power 12 minutes until rice is tender but firm. Continue as directed above.

Serves 6.
Prep Time: 10 minutes
Cook Time: 30 minutes

1 Gently fry onion, rice and mushrooms 5 minutes.

2 Rice will become a light brown colour.

CREAMY MUSHROOM PILAF

3 Stir in soup, water, wine and pepper.

4 Stir in sour cream and *half* of Parmesan cheese.

SAVOURY RICE

1 can	CAMPBELL'S condensed Consommé
300 ml	(*1/2 pt*) water
225 g	(*8 oz*) *uncooked* long-grain rice

In medium saucepan over moderate-high heat, heat consommé and water to simmer. Stir in rice. Reduce heat to low. Cover; simmer gently 20 minutes or until rice is tender and liquid is absorbed.

TIP: If liked, for added flavour, stir cooked, diced bacon or sliced, trimmed spring onions into cooked rice.

Serves 6.
Prep Time: 5 minutes
Cook Time: 25 minutes

SHORTCUT BEEF GRAVY

40 g	(*1 1/2 oz*) butter *or* margarine
45 ml	(*3 tbsp*) plain flour
1 can	CAMPBELL'S condensed Consommé
150 ml	(*1/4 pt*) water

In medium saucepan over moderate heat, melt butter; add flour. Cook 1 minute, stirring regularly. Gradually stir in consommé and water. Cook until gravy simmers and thickens, stirring regularly.

Serves 6 to 8.
Prep Time: 5 minutes
Cook Time: 5 minutes

$\mathcal{V}$EGETABLE COUSCOUS

1 can	**CAMPBELL'S condensed Consommé**
275 g	(*10 oz*) **uncooked couscous**
30 ml	(*2 tbsp*) **vegetable oil**
1	**medium onion, chopped**
100 g	(*4 oz*) **grated, peeled carrots**
75 g	(*3 oz*) **button mushrooms, wiped and sliced**
5 ml	(*1 tsp*) **grated fresh root ginger**
2	**cloves garlic, peeled and crushed**
15 ml	(*1 tbsp*) **soy sauce**
15 ml	(*1 tbsp*) **lemon juice**

■ In medium saucepan over high heat, bring consommé to simmer. Remove from heat. Stir in couscous. Cover; let stand 5 minutes.

■ Meanwhile, in large frying pan over moderate heat, in hot oil, gently fry onion, carrots, mushrooms, ginger and garlic until vegetables are softened, stirring regularly. Stir in soy sauce and lemon juice.

■ Add couscous. Heat through.

TIP: Reheat leftover vegetable couscous in your microwave oven. Stir in 15 or 30 ml (*1 or 2 tbsp*) water, if needed.

Serves 6 to 8.
Prep Time: 15 minutes
Cook Time: 15 minutes

Bulgur with basil and walnuts

1 can	**CAMPBELL'S condensed Consommé**
150 ml	(*¼ pt*) water
1	**medium onion, chopped**
100 g	(*4 oz*) **grated, peeled carrots**
25 g	(*1 oz*) **butter** *or* **margarine**
5 ml	(*1 tsp*) **dried basil**
1	**clove garlic, peeled and crushed**
225 g	(*8 oz*) *uncooked* **bulgur wheat**
25 g	(*1 oz*) **shelled walnuts, chopped**
15 ml	(*1 tbsp*) **lemon juice**

■ In medium saucepan over moderate heat, combine consommé, water, onion, carrots, butter, basil and garlic. Heat to simmer.

■ Add bulgur, walnuts and lemon juice. Simmer gently for 15 minutes or until bulgur is tender and liquid is absorbed.

Serves 6 to 8.
Prep Time: 10 minutes
Cook Time: 20 minutes

Mushroom, pepper and onion sauce

15 ml	(*1 tbsp*) **vegetable oil**
1	**onion, cut into wedges**
1 can	**CAMPBELL'S condensed Mushroom & Peppers Soup**
150 ml	(*¼ pt*) **water**
1.2 ml	(*¼ tsp*) **dried thyme**

■ In small saucepan over moderate heat, in hot oil, gently fry onion until softened.

■ Stir in soup, water and thyme. Simmer gently 5 minutes. Serve over grilled steak.

Serves 4 to 6.
Prep Time: 5 minutes
Cook Time: 10 minutes

BULGUR WITH BASIL AND WALNUTS

CURRIED PEANUT RICE

30 ml	(*2 tbsp*) vegetable oil
3	spring onions, trimmed and sliced
10 ml	(*2 tsp*) curry powder
1 can	CAMPBELL'S condensed Consommé
50 g	(*2 oz*) frozen peas
225 g	(*8 oz*) easy-cook, long-grain rice
50 g	(*2 oz*) roasted peanuts, roughly chopped

■ In medium saucepan over moderate heat, in hot oil, gently fry spring onions and curry powder until onions are softened, stirring occasionally.

■ Add consommé and peas. Heat to simmer. Add rice. Cover; simmer gently 15 minutes or until rice is tender and most of liquid is absorbed. Stir in peanuts. Fluff with fork before serving.

Serves 4 to 5.
Prep Time: 10 minutes
Cook Time: 25 minutes

MUSHROOMS IN GARLIC SAUCE

30 ml	(*2 tbsp*) olive oil
1	medium onion, sliced
4	cloves garlic, peeled and crushed
2.5 ml	(*¹/₂ tsp*) chopped fresh rosemary *or* 1.2 ml (*¹/₄ tsp*) dried rosemary
1.2 ml	(*¹/₄ tsp*) dried thyme
675 g	(*1¹/₂ lb*) closed cup mushrooms, wiped and thinly sliced
1 can	CAMPBELL'S condensed Consommé
5 ml	(*1 tsp*) lime *or* lemon juice
60 ml	(*4 tbsp*) dry white wine *or* dry sherry
	Chopped fresh parsley

■ In large saucepan over moderate heat, in hot oil, gently fry onion, garlic, rosemary and thyme until onion is softened.

■ Increase heat to moderate-high. Add mushrooms. Gently fry until mushrooms begin to brown. Add consommé and lime juice. Heat to simmer. Reduce heat to low. Simmer gently until mushrooms are tender, stirring occasionally.

■ Add wine. Simmer gently 3 minutes. Sprinkle with parsley. Garnish with fresh *rosemary* and *lime slice*, if liked. Serve with meat, rice or noodles.

Serves 6.
Prep Time: 15 minutes
Cook Time: 20 to 25 minutes

$\mathcal{M}$USHROOM MORNAY SAUCE

1 can	**CAMPBELL'S condensed Cream of Mushroom Soup**
175 ml	**(*6 fl oz*) milk**
1.2 ml	**(*¼ tsp*) mustard powder**
1	**(size 3) egg**
50 g	**(*2 oz*) Emmental cheese, grated**
15 ml	**(*1 tbsp*) grated Parmesan cheese**
	Freshly cooked vegetables

■ In small saucepan, stir soup; stir in milk and mustard until well combined. Over moderate heat, heat through, stirring occasionally.

■ In small jug, lightly beat egg. Stir some hot soup mixture into egg. Stir egg mixture back into soup.

■ Over low heat, simmer gently until mixture thickens, stirring regularly. *Do not boil.* Remove from heat. Stir in Emmental cheese and Parmesan cheese. Simmer gently until cheese melts. Serve over vegetables.

Makes about 500 ml (17 fl oz).
Prep Time: 10 minutes
Cook Time: 15 minutes

1 Pour soup into saucepan and stir. Stir in milk and mustard until well combined

2 Simmer gently over moderate heat, stirring occasionally.

3 Beat egg in small jug and add some of hot soup mixture.

4 Stir egg mixture back into soup mixture in saucepan.

VEGETABLE LASAGNE

1 can	**CAMPBELL'S condensed Cream of Celery Soup**
150 ml	**(¼ pt) milk**
100 g	**(4 oz) broccoli florets**
100 g	**(4 oz) courgettes, trimmed and sliced**
1 jar (475 g)	**(17 oz) tomato sauce for pasta**
1 can (198 g)	**(7 oz) sweetcorn, drained**
1	**green pepper, de-seeded and diced**
75 to 100 g	**(3 to 4 oz) no pre-cook dried lasagne sheets**
100 g	**(4 oz) Cheddar cheese, grated**

■ Preheat oven to 200 °C (*400 °F, gas mark 6*). In small bowl, combine soup and milk; set aside.

■ In medium saucepan, over moderate-high heat, in boiling water, simmer broccoli and courgettes 3 minutes. Drain; return to saucepan. Stir in tomato sauce, sweetcorn and green pepper.

■ Spoon ½ of vegetable mixture into 1.75-Lt (*3-pt*) rectangular ovenproof dish. Top with ½ of lasagne sheets and ½ of soup mixture. Repeat layers ending with soup mixture. Sprinkle with Cheddar cheese. Bake 30 minutes or until golden brown and bubbling.

Serves 4 to 5.
Prep Time: 15 minutes
Cook Time: 35 minutes

CAULIFLOWER AND BROCCOLI BAKE

CAULIFLOWER AND BROCCOLI BAKE

350 g	(*12 oz*) **fresh** *or* **frozen cauliflower florets**
175 g	(*6 oz*) **fresh** *or* **frozen broccoli florets**
1 can	**CAMPBELL'S condensed Ham & Cheese Soup**
150 ml	(*¼ pt*) **milk**
75 g	(*3 oz*) **Cheddar cheese, grated**
	Salt *and* **ground black pepper**

■ Preheat oven to 200 °C (*400 °F, gas mark 6*).

■ In medium saucepan over moderate heat, in 2.5 cm (*1 in*) boiling water, simmer cauliflower and broccoli 5 minutes or until just tender. Drain. Meanwhile, in small bowl, combine soup, milk and *50 g* (*2 oz*) *Cheddar cheese*. Season to taste with salt and pepper.

■ In shallow 1.75-Lt (*3-pt*) ovenproof dish, arrange vegetables. Pour soup mixture over vegetables. Sprinkle with remaining Cheddar cheese. Bake 20 to 25 minutes or until cheese is golden brown.

Serves 4 to 6.
Prep Time: 10 minutes
Cook Time: 30 to 35 minutes

VEGETABLES WITH LEMON SAUCE

1.5 kg	(*3 lb*) small red potatoes, scrubbed and quartered
150 g	(*5 oz*) broccoli florets
1	large red pepper, de-seeded and cut into 1-cm (*1/2-in*) slices
1 can	CAMPBELL's condensed Cream of Celery *or* Cream of Mushroom Soup
100 ml	(*4 fl oz*) mayonnaise
3	spring onions, trimmed and chopped
15 ml	(*1 tbsp*) lemon juice
1.2 ml	(*1/4 tsp*) dried tarragon

■ In large saucepan place potatoes; add water to cover. Over high heat, heat to boiling. Reduce heat to low. Cover; simmer 15 minutes or until tender. Drain; keep warm. Set aside.

■ In same saucepan over moderate heat, in 2.5 cm (*1 in*) boiling water, simmer broccoli and red pepper 5 minutes or until tender. Drain. Arrange potatoes, broccoli and red pepper on serving plate.

■ Meanwhile, in medium saucepan over moderate heat, combine soup, mayonnaise, onions, lemon juice and tarragon. Heat through, stirring occasionally. Pour over vegetables.

Serves 6 to 8.
Prep Time: 10 minutes
Cook Time: 25 to 30 minutes

VEGETABLES WITH LEMON SAUCE

VEGETABLE CURRY

15 ml	(*1 tbsp*) vegetable oil
1	medium onion, thinly sliced
1 can	CAMPBELL'S condensed Creamy Vegetable Soup
300 ml	(*¹/₂ pt*) water
45 ml	(*3 tbsp*) mild curry paste
175 g	(*6 oz*) thickly sliced, peeled carrots
175 g	(*6 oz*) cauliflower florets
100 g	(*4 oz*) frozen peas

■ In large saucepan over moderate heat, in hot oil, gently fry onion 5 minutes or until softened.

■ Stir in soup, water and curry paste. Add carrots and cauliflower. Simmer gently 25 minutes or until carrots are just tender, stirring occasionally. Add peas and simmer gently 5 minutes, stirring regularly.

Serves 4.
Prep Time: 10 minutes
Cook Time: 40 minutes

CREAMY VEGETABLE MEDLEY

1 can	**CAMPBELL'S condensed Cream of Celery *or* Cream of Mushroom Soup**
150 ml	**(*¼ pt*) water**
1 pkt (450 g)	**(*1 lb*) frozen mixed vegetables (e.g. courgettes, broccoli, carrots and cauliflower)**

■ In medium saucepan, combine soup and water. Over moderate heat, heat to simmer. Stir in vegetables.

■ Return to simmer. Reduce heat to low. Cover; simmer gently 10 minutes or until vegetables are tender, stirring occasionally.

To microwave: In 2-Lt (*3½-pt*) microwave-proof dish, combine soup and vegetables. Cover; microwave on HIGH 10 minutes or until vegetables are tender, stirring halfway through cooking. Let stand covered, 5 minutes.

Serves 6.
Prep Time: 5 minutes
Cook Time: 15 minutes

QUICK CHICKEN RISOTTO

25 g	(*1 oz*) **butter** *or* **margarine**
225 g	(*8 oz*) **boneless chicken breasts** *or* **thighs, skinned and cut into 1-cm** (*¹/₂-in*) **strips**
1	**small onion, finely chopped**
1	**small red pepper, de-seeded and finely diced**
225 g	(*8 oz*) **easy-cook, long-grain rice**
1 can	**CAMPBELL'S condensed Cream of Mushroom** *or* **Chicken & Mushroom Soup**
600 ml	(*1 pt*) **water**
1	**chicken stock cube, crumbled**
100 g	(*4 oz*) **frozen peas**
	Salt *and* **ground black pepper**

■ In large saucepan over moderate heat, in hot butter, gently fry chicken, onion and red pepper about 5 minutes or until chicken is lightly browned and vegetables are softened, stirring regularly.

■ Add rice, gently fry 30 seconds, stirring regularly. Stir in soup, water and stock cube. Heat to simmer.

■ Simmer, uncovered, 15 minutes stirring occasionally. Add peas; simmer gently 5 minutes more or until rice and chicken are tender and liquid is absorbed, stirring regularly. Season to taste with salt and pepper.

Quick Risotto: Prepare Quick Chicken Risotto as directed above, *except* omit the chicken.

Serves 4 to 5.
Prep Time: 10 minutes
Cook Time: 30 minutes

QUICK CHICKEN RISOTTO

CREAMY POTATO SALAD

1.5 kg	(*3 lb*) medium potatoes, peeled and cubed
1 can	CAMPBELL'S condensed Cream of Celery Soup
175 ml	(*6 fl oz*) mayonnaise
30 ml	(*2 tbsp*) red wine vinegar
100 g	(*4 oz*) chopped, trimmed celery
4	spring onions, trimmed and chopped
1	small green pepper, de-seeded and diced
2	(size 3) hard-boiled eggs, shelled and chopped

■ In large saucepan, place potatoes; add water to cover. Over high heat, heat to boiling. Reduce heat to low. Cover; simmer 10 to 15 minutes or until tender. Drain. Cool slightly.

■ In large bowl, combine soup, mayonnaise and vinegar.

■ Add potatoes, celery, spring onions, green pepper and eggs; toss gently to coat. Cover; refrigerate at least 4 hours before serving.

Serves 8.
Prep Time: 20 minutes
Cook Time: 20 to 25 minutes
Chill Time: 4 hours

CREAMY BAKED MACARONI

275 g	(*10 oz*) dried macaroni
1 can	CAMPBELL'S condensed Cream of Chicken *or* Ham & Cheese Soup
300 ml	(*1/2 pt*) milk
15 ml	(*1 tbsp*) chopped fresh chives
2.5 ml	(*1/4 tsp*) mustard powder
1.2 ml	(*1/4 tsp*) Tabasco sauce
225 g	(*8 oz*) Gouda cheese cut in 1-cm (*1/2-in*) cubes

■ Preheat oven to 200 °C (*400 °F, gas mark 6*). Cook macaroni according to packet directions. Drain.

■ In 2-Lt (*3 1/2-pt*) casserole, combine soup, milk, chives, mustard and Tabasco sauce. Stir in macaroni and *half* of Gouda cheese. Sprinkle with remaining Gouda cheese. Bake 15 to 20 minutes or until golden brown and bubbling.

Serves 4 to 6.
Prep Time: 20 minutes
Cook Time: 15 to 20 minutes

CREAMY POTATO SALAD

TAGLIATELLE CARBONARA

225 g	(*8 oz*) dried tagliatelle
1 can	CAMPBELL'S condensed Ham & Cheese Soup
150 ml	(*¼ pt*) milk *or* dry white wine
100 g	(*4 oz*) ham, finely diced
30 ml	(*2 tbsp*) chopped fresh parsley
	Salt *and* ground black pepper

■ In large saucepan, cook tagliatelle according to packet directions. Drain.

■ In same saucepan, combine soup and milk. Add tagliatelle, ham and parsley. Over low heat, simmer gently, tossing and stirring regularly 5 minutes or until heated through. Season to taste with salt and pepper.

Quick Pasta Sauce: In small saucepan, combine soup and milk. Over moderate heat, gently heat through, stirring regularly. Season to taste with salt and pepper. Toss freshly cooked pasta with soup mixture.

Serves 4.
Prep Time: 5 minutes
Cook Time: 15 to 20 minutes

CREAMY POTATO BAKE

1 can	**CAMPBELL'S condensed Cream of Celery Soup**
150 ml	**(*¼ pt*) milk**
5 ml	**(*1 tsp*) garlic granules (optional)**
	Salt *and* ground black pepper
575 g	**(*1¼ lb*) potatoes, peeled and thinly sliced**
1	**small onion, thinly sliced**
50 g	**(*2 oz*) Cheddar cheese, grated**
	Fresh parsley sprig for garnish

■ Preheat oven to 200 °C (*400 °F, gas mark 6*). In small bowl, combine soup, milk and garlic. Season to taste with salt and pepper.

■ In 1.15-Lt (*2-pt*) ovenproof dish, arrange alternate layers of potatoes, onion and soup mixture. Sprinkle with Cheddar cheese. Bake 45 to 55 minutes or until potatoes are tender and topping is golden brown. Garnish with parsley, if liked.

TIP: If liked, you can make this casserole with sliced, scrubbed potatoes.

Serves 4 to 6.
Prep Time: 15 minutes
Cook Time: 45 to 55 minutes

SPECIAL MAC 'N' CHEESE BAKE

225 g	**(*8 oz*) dried macaroni**
1 can	**CAMPBELL'S condensed Ham & Cheese Soup**
200 ml	**(*7 fl oz*) milk**
75 g	**(*3 oz*) Cheddar cheese, grated**

■ Preheat oven to 200 °C (*400 °F, gas mark 6*).

■ Cook macaroni according to packet directions. Drain.

■ In 1.4-Lt (*2½-pt*) ovenproof dish, combine soup and milk. Stir in macaroni and *50 g (2 oz)* Cheddar cheese. Sprinkle with remaining Cheddar cheese. Bake 25 minutes or until golden brown and bubbling.

Serves 4 to 6.
Prep Time: 20 minutes
Cook Time: 25 minutes

$\mathcal{E}$ASY TURKEY SALAD

1 can	**CAMPBELL'S condensed Mushroom & Peppers Soup**
100 ml	**(*4 fl oz*) mayonnaise**
575 g	**(*1¼ lb*) chopped, cooked turkey *or* chicken**
100 g	**(*4 oz*) finely chopped, trimmed celery**
3	**spring onions, trimmed and sliced**
30 ml	**(*2 tbsp*) chopped fresh parsley**
	Pinch ground black pepper
	Lettuce leaves

■ In large bowl, combine soup and mayonnaise. Stir in turkey, celery, onions, parsley and pepper.

■ Serve mixture on lettuce leaves.

Serves 6 to 8.
Prep Time: 20 minutes

STROGANOFF SAUCE

15 g	(*½ oz*) butter *or* margarine
1	small onion, chopped
1 can	CAMPBELL'S condensed Cream of Mushroom Soup
75 ml	(*3 fl oz*) sour cream
60 ml	(*4 tbsp*) milk
1.2 ml	(*¼ tsp*) paprika

■ In small saucepan over moderate heat, in hot butter, gently fry onion until softened. Stir in soup, sour cream, milk and paprika. Gently heat through, stirring regularly.

■ Serve over cooked vegetables, beef or rice.

To microwave: Reduce butter to 7 g (*¼ oz*). In small microwave-proof dish, combine butter and onion. Cover; microwave on HIGH 3 minutes or until onion is softened, stirring halfway through cooking. Stir in soup, sour cream, milk and paprika. Cover; microwave on HIGH 3 minutes or until hot, stirring halfway through cooking. Serve as directed above.

Makes about 450 ml (¾ pt).
Prep Time: 5 minutes
Cook Time: 10 minutes

CREAMY CELERY SAUCE

1 can	CAMPBELL'S condensed Cream of Celery Soup
150 ml	(*¼ pt*) milk
	Salt *and* ground black pepper

■ In small saucepan, combine soup and milk. Over moderate heat, gently heat through, stirring regularly. Season to taste with salt and pepper.

■ Serve over cooked vegetables.

Makes 450 ml (¾ pt).
Prep Time: 5 minutes
Cook Time: 5 minutes

SOUPER SAUCE FOR ROAST MEAT OR POULTRY

30 to 60 ml	(*2 to 4 tbsp*) roasted meat *or* poultry drippings in pan
1 can	CAMPBELL'S condensed Cream of Mushroom *or* Cream of Chicken Soup
45 to 75 ml	(*3 to 5 tbsp*) water

■ After roasting meat or poultry, remove roast from pan. Spoon off excess fat, reserving 30 to 60 ml (*2 to 4 tbsp*) drippings. Stir in soup and water. Over moderate heat, gently heat through, stirring to loosen browned bits.

■ Serve with roast meat or poultry.

Makes about 350 ml (½ pt).
Prep Time: 5 minutes
Cook Time: 5 minutes

EASY BARBECUE SAUCE

1 can	CAMPBELL'S condensed Cream of Tomato Soup
1	small onion, chopped
60 ml	(*4 tbsp*) Worcestershire sauce
45 ml	(*3 tbsp*) malt vinegar
30 ml	(*2 tbsp*) light brown soft sugar

■ In small saucepan, combine soup, onion, Worcestershire sauce, vinegar and sugar. Over moderate heat, heat to simmer. Reduce heat to low. Simmer gently 10 minutes, stirring regularly.

■ Use to baste beef or chicken during grilling or barbecuing.

Makes about 450 ml (¾ pt).
Prep Time: 5 minutes
Cook Time: 15 minutes

MUSHROOM AND PEPPER SAUCE

1 can	**CAMPBELL'S condensed Mushroom & Peppers Soup**
150 ml	**(¼ pt) milk**
	Salt *and* ground black pepper

■ In small saucepan, combine soup and milk. Over moderate heat, gently heat through, stirring regularly. Season to taste with salt and pepper.

■ Serve over grilled or fried pork chops, lamb chops or chicken.

Makes 450 ml (¾ pt).
Prep Time: 5 minutes
Cook Time: 5 minutes